Computer Applications for Journalism

Rahul Singhai

Reference Press

4831/24, Ansari Road,
Darya Ganj,
New Delhi-110 002.
Phone: 51563444, 23260807
Fax: 51563334
E-mail: info@essessreference.com
url: www.essessreference.com

First Published : 2006

Rs.550/-

ISBN: 81-8405-008-9

Published By:
Reference Press
4831/24, Ansari Road,
Darya Ganj,
New Delhi-110 002.
Phone: 23260807, 51563444
Fax: 51563334
E-mail: info@essessreference.com
url: www.essessreference.com

Printed in India at:
Mehra Offset Press, New Delhi.

Contents

Preface

Advances in computer applications and information systems have created new opportunities as well as challenges to the journalism resources. In the past two decades or so, information has become a key issue of interest to both researchers and practitioners since the advent of computers. The issue has become more of a concern and a challenge to both communities with the tremendous advances in computer applications and information systems in recent times. The heightened concern and challenge is, in part, due to the tremendous amount of information generated with the advancement of computer technology and journalism issues.

Information support systems are designed in a way to help solve some of the concerns and challenges of managing information resources. These systems provide the tools and means of managing information resources on persons, groups, and organizations. Without doubt, support systems are key topics for current and future research efforts aimed at maximizing the management of information resources introduces electronic journalism as a new trend in the news services that have recently been boosted by Internet diffusion.

Author

1

Introduction to Computers

We are living in an information age dependent upon digital information. Digital information is electronic information, the result of computer processing. Every type of job relies upon getting information, using it, managing it, and relaying information to others. Computers enable the efficient processing and storage of information.

Computer is an electronic device that can perform the following tasks:

— Respond to input.

— Process that input according to a set of instructions.

— Store the instructions and the results of processing.

— Output information.

The input-processing-output cycle is called the throughput process.

Types of Computers

— Mainframe — large-scale computers used to process large volumes of data.

— Minicomputer — computers that are physically smaller and cost far less than mainframes, yet are powerful enough to do many of the jobs that only the big mainframes could do before.

— Microcomputer — a smaller and cheaper personal computer built around a microprocessor. By far the most widely used computer today, available in desktop or laptop models.

Hardware Components

— Keyboard and Mouse.

— Display Screen.

— Processor Unit.

— Disks and Disk Drives

— Printer

Computer Literacy

A person who is computer literate should be able:

— To see the broad range of computer application in all areas of academic and professional life today.

— To appreciate the positive and negative effects of the computer revolution on the modern world, the so-called "computers and society" issues.

— To grasp fundamental concepts of computer hardware, software, and their connection to people, the third element of the Computer Triangle.

— To become familiar with a variety of applications software programs currently used with microcomputers, including word processing, spreadsheets, databases, and computer graphics, and to understand how to apply them for personal and scholarly purposes.

— To examine the fast-developing frontier of the Internet, sometimes called the Information Superhighway, to understand how it will change the ways people receive and access information.

— To identify emerging trends in computing, including artificial intelligence, to convey a sense of how the machine will continue to affect our lives in the future.

MULTIMEDIA AND THE INTERNET

— CD-ROM encyclopedias.

— Computer mapping.

— The World Wide Web.

Hypertext and Multimedia

— *Hypertext*: A computer application that integrates at least one medium with text, such as more text, sound, or graphics.

— *Multimedia*: Integrating all media together in one computer application with some kind of navigation system between them creates a multimedia application.

Monitor

The Computer Monitor is the computer user's window into the workings of the computer. It consists of a television picture tube that had been modified to accept the type of video signal created by the computer's electronics. Conventional televisions can be used as computer monitors if a tranlation device is used to connect them. The picture quality leaves something to be desired.

Keyboard

The Keyboard is the primary input device used to communicate with the computer. A computer keyboard closely resembles a conventional typewriter keyboard with the addition of numerous keys that are used specifically for computing functions.

Mouse

Named for the resemblance of the wire coming out of it and a mouse's tail, the mouse was introduced to computing in the early 1980's when Macintosh created its graphical user interface (GUI). The mouse is another input device used to point at objects on the computer monitor and select them. Using the mouse and keyboard in combination allows the computer user substantial latitude in how to accomplish a wide variety of tasks.

Floppy Diskette Drive

Once the most advanced of storage devices, floppy diskettes are normally used a temporary storage containers or transportation media for data. A standard floppy diskette can hold 1.44 MB of computer data. This amounts to a rather large number of pages if translated to the paper standard for textual information. Computer diskettes are not as reliable or fast as the internal storage drives on the computer. They are also the primary vector of virus infection in the computer world.

CD-ROM Drive

This modern miracle gained prominence in the late 1980's and has become the primary distribution medium for software to consumers. The Compact Disk-Read Only Memory (CD-ROM) disk itself is a collection of concentric circles containing millions of pits and plateaus which correspond to on/off bits of data. The disk is read with an optical laser similar to the one used to scan your groceries at the supermarket. Most disks of this kind are "Read Only" meaning that the computer can retrieve information from the disk, but cannot place information on it. New developments have improved this technology to allow writing and rewriting data to the disk. A different kind of hardware mechanism is needed to employ this innovation.

Computer Peripherals

Computer peripherals are any electronic devices that can be hooked up to a computer other than the standard input-output devices (monitor, keyboard,mouse). Peripheral devices include speakers, microphones, printers, scanners, digital cameras, plotters, and modems. Peripherals often require special software packages called "drivers". These drivers are usually included with the peripheral at purchase time.

Like all things man-made, computers have evolved a lexicon all their own. The following incomplete list should help alleviate misunderstandings of computer-related terms:

CD-ROM: CD-ROM disks are becoming the standard for delivering programs from the software developer to the computer user. CD-ROM's come in a variety of flavors based on the language they are written in (PC, Mac, or Unix). PC's cannot read a Mac CD-ROM, but Macs can read PC CD-ROMS.

CPU: The brain of the computer. This is located on a circuit board inside the desktop or tower computer case. This component has terms associated with it such as "486", "Pentium" and "Celeron". Most of the CPU's are manufactured by a company called Intel. They are the Microsoft of the hardware world.

Data: Computer food. Data can be numbers, letters, symbols, mathematical expressions, mouse clicks, or button presses. The CPU translates all this activity to series of zeroes and ones and then performs magic.

Drivers: Drivers are software packages that are needed to run certain peripheral devices. Printers, monitors, scanners, and network cards all require software drivers so that the computer knows how to communicate and control the device.

486: An older CPU that was constructed at the beginning of the Windows 95 revolution. This CPU works great if you are running MS-DOS or Windows 3.1. In general, this is one of the things that should be considered when purchasing a computer.

Hard Disk Drive (HDD): This is the internal magnetic storage device housed inside the computer case. These come in a variety of sizes, measured in how many bits of information they can contain. A bit of information equals either zero (0) or one (1). To a computer, this is equivalent to turning a light switch off (0) or on (1). Computers operate on bits in groups of 8, called a byte. Every byte contains 8 bits. Bits and bytes can be stored magnetically on material that resembles cassette or 8-track recording tape. The magnetic material stores information as sequences of the digits "0" and "1" (hence the name digital storage).

Since it takes many bytes to store such things as letters, words, and sentences, the amount of information that a Hard Drive can store is measured in multiples of 1000-bytes, 1,000,000 bytes, or 1,000,000,000 bytes. Terms such as kilobyte (1000 bytes or 1KB), megabyte (1,000,000 bytes or 1MB), and gigabyte (1,000,000,000 bytes or 1GB) have evolved to represent these storage capacities. When you purchase a computer, get as large a Hard Drive as you can afford. The standard in 1998 was between 4GB and 8GB. The Hard Disk Drive is often referred to as the "C:" drive.

Floppy Diskette: The floppy diskette is a removable storage device that is used by the Floppy Diskette Drive (also known as the A: drive or FDD). This storage device is capable of holding 1,440,000 bytes (1.44MB) of data. The Floppy Diskette is inserted and removed from a slotted opening on the front of the computer case.

Keyboard: The main tool to get information into the computer and the most common way to tell the computer what you want it to do. Most keyboards have the same arrangement of keys as a typical typewriter keyboard. Computer keyboards have additional keys that perform computer-specific functions.

Modem: A telecommunications peripheral device that allows computer to communicate with one another via conventional telephone lines. Modems are required for home computers to access the Internet or to send and receive facsimile transmissions (FAX). Modems are rated by their speed in moving data from the computer to the telephone line. This speed is measured in bits per second (bps). Standard modern modems are rated at 28,800 bps, 33,600 bps and 56,400 bps.

Monitor: The "Television" screen that allows you to see what the computer is doing. Many newcomers to computing mistakenly think of the monitor as the computer itself. Computers can operate without a monitor, but computer users cannot.

Motherboard: The circuit board on which most of the major electronic components are situated. Most manufacturers integrate cable attachment ports on the back-end of the motherboard. They also include slots so that owners can add their own cable attachment ports. The slots are designed to accept cards. These are normally found near the back of the computer case.

Mouse: A common input device used to tell a computer what it needs to do. With the invention of the Macintosh and Windows operating systems, computer users needed a device to point at objects on the screen and select them.

MS-DOS: An older operating system that powered personal computers through their beginning years. Prior to the development of the graphics-oriented Macintosh and Windows operating systems, this system relied on typing commands one line at a time to tell the computer what you wanted it to do. This system is still in use in the Windows family of software and still has many practical uses. Windows 3.1 relies on MS-DOS to operate. MS-DOS stands for Microsoft-Disk Operating System.

Network Card: A card that can be installed in one of the motherboard slots to give the computer the ability to talk to other computers with similar cards. A collection of similarly equipped computers connected by specially designed cables is known as a network. The mechanism (including languages and protocols) used to communicate on a network are varied, but the most common networking designs in use are Ethernet and Token Ring.

Operating System Software (OS): The instructions that allow the computer to start working and permit it to run other programs. The major OS software types include MS-DOS, Windows 3.1, Windows 95, Windows NT, Macintosh, UNIX, and LINUX. The most popular OS in use at present is Windows 95. Most computers come with one of these pre-installed.

Platform: The computer operating system and/or architecture. Computers that are capable of running MS-

DOS, Windows 3.1 or Windows95/NT operating system software typically have the Intel 486/Pentium CPU. Computers running the Macintosh operating system software have a Motorola 68xxx/PowerPC CPU. For the most part, these platforms are incompatible as they have different rules and instructions for performing their tasks.

Pentium - Pentium II: Faster, larger CPU devices that are designed to allow more computing instructions to occur per second. Most computers manufactured in the past 3 to 4 years contain this device.

Peripheral Device: Any device that is connected to the computer in addition to the basic CPU-Monitor-Keyboard-Mouse configuration. External speakers, microphones, joysticks, printers, and scanners are examples of peripherals.

Printer: A peripheral device that allows the computer user to produce paper copies of the information processed by the computer. Common home printers spray ink on paper and are called ink-jet printers. Office and school printers are typically laser printers which work on the same principle as a xerographic copy machine, using electrostatic charges and toner cartridges to place information on paper.

Program: A complex set of instructions that allow the computer user to process data. Common programs include word-processing, spreadsheets, databases, drawing and painting, Internet tools, and games. Programs are necessary for computers to be useful to humans.

RAM: This acronym stands for Random Access Memory. RAM is commonly called "memory". Memory is measured in megabytes (MB) and usually comes in multiples of 2 or 4. The more RAM that a computer has, the better it can carry out instructions. It is recommended that a new computer have 32 MB, 64MB, or 128MB of RAM.

Hooking Up a Computer

Computers are getting relatively easy to hook up. The computer owner used to have to keep a technical manual at his or her side to make sure which wire connects to which port. Each of the peripheral devices has a cable that needs to be connected to the back of the computer. Most of these cables have a special connector type that is designed to fit one and only one type of port. You may hear or read about "serial" ports, "parallel" ports, 25-pin connectors, 9-pin connectors and the like. Each of these descriptors refers to a special wiring configuration. Each of the connectors normally fits one and only one port on the back of the computer.

Both the CPU housing and the monitor will have conventional household power cords. These are the 3-prong variety and it is strongly recommended that you plug the computer and monitor into a grounded outlet instead of using the 2-prong converter (or just cutting the grounding prong off). It is also recommended that you purchase a high quality, grounded, multi-outlet power strip that offers a good measure of surge protection. During an electrical storm, the best thing you can do for your computer is to unplug it from the power source. Most insurance claims on electrically damaged computer equipment results from lightning damage that originated from the telephone line connected to the modem. It is a wise computer owner who not only "unplugs" his computer, but disconnects the phone line, as well.

Most new computers come with simple, easy to follow instructions for connecting the cables. If you ever plan to detach the cables and move the computer to a new location, it would be wise to get out a few bottles of colored nail polish and paint some identifying marks on the cables and above the ports so that you can easily tell which wire belongs in which socket. Many manufacturers are beginning to color-code their connectors to make setting up the computer easier.

Disk Drives

In the early days of computing, information storage was done on magnetic tape, similar to VCR or cassette tape. The disadvantage of using tape as a storage device was that it could not be accessed randomly. In other words, if information was stored midway on the tape, the tape would have to be forwarded or rewound to that position before the information could be retrieved. The first Radio Shack TRS-80's could have a cassette tape player hooked to them and could then store information. It was necessary for the user to write down the tape recorder's counter position whenever a new set of data was stored.

This primitive means of storing and retrieving data was soon replaced by the 5.25-inch floppy disk. The wonderful thing about this disk was that the computer itself kept track of where the information was stored and could access information from anywhere on the disk very rapidly. The large floppy disk (named because of its flexibility) was replaced by the 3.5-inch plastic shielded diskette which proved to be more durable and small enough to fit in a shirt pocket. The large floppy disk could hold about 360 KB of information while the diskette could hold up to 1.44 MB. New diskette drive designs (called Superdrives) allow as much as 120 MB of storage on a single disk!

The workhorse of the modern PC is the hard disk drive (HDD). A hard disk drive consists of a set of stacked metal platters coated on both sides with a magnetic recording material. The platters are read by magnetic reading heads, each resembling the tone-arm of a record player. The more platters and reading heads built into the drive, the larger the storage capacity. The HDD stores the operating instructions needed by the computer to start up and run properly. It is vital to keep the HDD working properly in order for the computer to remain healthy. The dreaded "Computer Crash" normally occurs whenever the hard disk drive fails to work.

Maintaining the integrity of data on a HDD has become an industry in itself. Computers can have more than one HDD and more than one diskette drive. The HDD is normally referred to as the "C: Drive" while the diskette drive is commonly referred to as the "A: Drive". A second diskette drive is usually designated as the "B: Drive". Additional hard disk drives will be given different drive labels, such as "F: Drive", "G: Drive", etc. On a network, other storage devices can be "mapped" and used as storage devices by the local computer. These drives will also be assigned letters.

Other drives attached to the computer (such as CD-ROM Drives, Zip Drives, Jaz Drives and SCSI Drives) are assigned additional drive letters so that the computer operator and the computer can keep track of where the data will be coming from or going to. The more complex the machine, the more complex its maintenance.

Uses of Disk

— Checkdisk

— Scandisk

— Defragmenting (Optimizing)

— Formatting

— Partitioning

— Emergency- Contingency Plans

Checkdisk: Checkdisk is a holdover from the MS-DOS days of computer.

Scandisk: Scandisk is an MS-DOS utility that is incorporated into the Windows 95 operating system.

Defragmentation (Optimizing): After a disk has been used for a while, numerous writes and rewrites and erasures can separate data into bits and pieces scattered throughout a disk. Defragmenting or Optimizing a disk is a technique that takes pieces of information that have been written to separate regions of the disk and consolidates them into contiguous data units.

Formatting: In order to get a disk or diskette ready for use, you sometimes have to format it. Formatting involves erasing all the data from the disk, checking it for physical errors, removing bad sectors from the disk map, and generally preparing the disk to accept data from the particular computer system that it is being prepared for. There is no physical difference between a diskette that is used with a Macintosh, a PC, or a Unix computer. The difference lies in the way that disk is prepared or formatted.

To format a diskette, insert the diskette into the diskette drive slot, click on the Start Button, and select Run. In the dialogue box that appears, type the following: "format a:" (without the quotes). Pressing the ENTER key on the keyboard will begin the process of preparing the diskette for use on your computer. It takes approximately one minute to format a standard 3.5-inch diskette. All disks, at some time or other, are formatted prior to using them on a computer system. Be careful not to format your Hard Disk Drive unless you absolutely know what you are doing. Formatting the C: Drive will literally bring you to tears. This is best left to the experts and only whenever all else fails.

Partitioning: Hard Disks can be subdivided into smaller virtual areas (partitions) by means of partitioning. Whenever a hard disk is formatted, the formatting utility creates only a single disk partition. A DOS utility called FDISK can be used to subdivide a hard disk drive into sections. The purpose of doing this is to protect portions of the disk from a software crash. If the operating system is stored on one partition of the disk and the applications on another, if the operating system crashes and becomes corrupt, the software applications won't be affected by measure used to correct the operating system problems. The OS partition can be reformatted and the software reinstalled without affecting the software applications and data stored on the other partition.

Partitioning is something that is done by experienced users and should not be experimented with on your primary hard disk. The FDISK utility is a powerful tool. One of its most beneficial uses is to restore the Master Boot Partition (MBR) on a hard disk that has forgotten how to read its data. Some viruses attack the MBR and render the computer useless. If the user is able to boot from a diskette and read the hard drive from the MS-DOS prompt, then the FDISK command can be used to restore the MBR and bring the computer back to life. The command is "FDISK /MBR" (without the quotes). Use this command only when warranted.

Starting and Stopping a Computer

Like all electronic devices, the computer has an ON-OFF switch to bring power into it. You will find either a pushbutton switch located on the front of the CPU housing, or a toggle switch located on the back of the CPU housing. Chances are that the monitor and the computer are not powered by the same switch. It the monitor has an ON-OFF switch, it should be on before the CPU is brought to life. The same is true for any peripherals that the computer will be using. It is best to have them turned on so that the computer can find them as it runs through its start up instructions.

The operating system of a modern PC is very complex and may take over a minute or two to completely prepare itself for use. Be patient. Once the computer has completed the startup procedure, it is ready to take orders from its master....you! Most of what you will do with the computer after it starts can be accessed using the "Start" button at the lower left corner of the screen (in Windows 95).

When you are ready to stop using the computer, you must take it through a shutdown procedure.

Using the Mouse

Using the mouse takes a bit of hand-eye coordination. The mouse is set up to be used by right-handed people and is traditionally placed on the right side of the keyboard. A PC-based mouse will have 2 or 3 buttons while a Macintosh mouse will have only one. There is a ball inside the bottom of the mouse that rolls whenever you glide the mouse across a surface. As the ball rolls, it sends instructions to the computer telling it where to place the arrow on the computer screen.

Most of the time, the mouse is placed on a smooth, rubber-backed surface called a mousepad. While not necessary, a mousepad can make the movement of the mouse smoother and easier. The mouse ball can pick up dirt, dust, and oils from the surface that it is gliding over. These contaminants then gum up the internal rollers and cause the mouse to work improperly. Removing the ball and cleaning the rollers is a routine maintenance procedure. Keeping the mousepad clean also helps.

When the mouse is rolled across the table, the arrow on the screen moves in the same direction. If you move the mouse to the right, the arrow moves to the right. If you move the mouse forward, the arrow moves upward. Practice is the only way to become acclimated to using the mouse. If you run out of room on the mousepad or desktop, simply lift the mouse off the table and place it back in the center of your work area. As long as the mouseball is not touching a surface, the arrow won't move.

The mouse is used to point at and select items. Pointing involves moving the mouse until the arrow tip lies on top of the item on the screen that you wish to work with. Selecting involves clicking the left mouse button. There are two kinds of "clicks"... "single-clicks" and "double-clicks". Single-clicking (clicking the left button once) is used to select objects and make them active. Double-clicking (clicking the left button twice in rapid succession) is used to launch programs and cause computer actions. The general rule of thumb is, "if single-clicking doesn't work, try double-clicking".

Windows 95/98/NT makes use of the right button on the mouse. One of the most helpful tools that was included in the Windows95/98/NT OS was the ability to right-click on all kinds of objects to bring up choices of things that can be done with those objects. Right-clicking will make your computing tasks much easier to accomplish.

Installing Software

Most software that you purchase will be distributed on CD-ROM or Diskette Sets. If the software is distributed on CD-ROM, inserting the disk into the CD-ROM drive will probably launch the setup process. All you will have to do is watch the screen and agree to a few questions. The program will be automatically installed and additions will be made to the menuing system.

Software that is sold on diskette sets will not activate the self-installation procedures. You will have to do this manually. Follow these easy steps:

1. Insert the first diskette (Disk 1) in the diskette drive slot
2. Click the button and choose "Run" from the menu
3. Type "a:setup" (without quotes) and click on the OK button

The installation program will begin. If the program is distributed on more than one disk, the setup program will ask you to exchange disks periodically. Be sure that you insert the disk tha the program specifies.

Uninstalling

In the event that you wish to remove software from the computer, most commercial products build in an Uninstall routine when they are installed. To best method of accessing this routine is to open the Control Panel. Click the Start Button, move the mouse pointer upward until it is on top of the word "Settings". A submenu will appear that contains the Control Panel icon. Move your mouse to the right until the arrow is over the Control Panel Folder and then click the left mouse button once. Doing so will bring up the following screen:

Clicking the "Add/Remove Programs" icon will then allow you to uninstall software from a list. Carefully choose the software package that you want to remove and then click the "Add/Remove" button. The computer will take care of the rest. It is a really good idea to make sure that you don't have the program running on the computer when you try to uninstall it.

Most computers have an operating system installed when you purchase them. The most recent operating system installed on Intel-based machines is Windows 98. You can also buy computers that have Windows 95 or Windows NT installed instead (WinNT will cost you more). On the Macintosh side of the world, all current

Macs come with MacOS8 or a variant. You don't have much latitude when you purchase their products. Some computer distributors include additional software as a "bundle" when you purchase their product. Here is a recommended list of generic software that you might want start with:

Word Processor: There are numerous word processors available. Windows 95/98/NT comes with a nice little package preinstalled called "Wordpad". It is a scaled-down version of Microsoft's Word, a very powerful application. If you don't require spell-checking, grammar-checking, tables, columns, and the like, you might be able to get by with Wordpad. If you need something better, check our Microsoft's Word or Corel's Wordperfect.

Internet Software: Many computers ship with Microsoft's Internet Explorer and/or Netscape's Navigator. Both will allow you to explore the World Wide Web. Both packages also include an Email program. These are two of the most useful Internet applications. Depending on your computing needs, you might want to acquire a database/spreadsheet application, some games, financial packages, encyclopedias, and other useful applications. A good all-purpose program that you might give consideration to purchasing is Microsoft Works (or its competitor, Appleworks). If you wish to explore the world of desktop publishing, consider Microsoft Publisher'98. Both Works and Publisher are under $100 at your friendly retail software store

Operations of a Computer System

Input: Home computers are microcomputers. Input is supplied to the microcomputer with the use of a keyboard, a mouse, or another input device. These input devices may be called peripheral devices.

Processing: Processing is done inside the computer in an area called the central processing unit (CPU). Processing is the conversion of input to output.

Storage: Storage refers to holding information somewhere. RAM, Random Access Memory, is short-term memory. It is volatile memory because the memory is automatically "erased" when the power is turned off or interrupted. The RAM memory is located inside the computer case on the motherboard. A motherboard is not the keyboard. The keyboard is what you type with. A motherboard holds RAM memory, electronic circuits and other computer parts including the central processing unit. ROM, Read-Only-Memory, is not volatile meaning the memory is still there when power is interrupted or turned off. When the computer is turned back on again, ROM memory is still in storage on the internal hard disk.

Output: Output is the result of a computer process. Output may be viewed on a monitor screen, heard through speakers, printed on printers, and so forth. Output devices may be considered hardware and are also considered to be peripheral devices.

A computer system refers to the computer AND all of its equipment. Equipment like speakers, printer, keyboard, scanner, etc. is called peripheral equipment, sometimes shortened to "peripherals". The central processing unit (CPU) is considered to be "the computer". Without peripheral equipment (such as monitor, printer, speakers, etc.) for input and output the microcomputer (home computer) will not be able to do anything you find useful.

Your computer system cannot help you type a letter unless you have some type of software (program) to do this. Most typing is handled by a "word processing" program. A software program for your computer can be purchased at stores like Office Depot, Staples, and computer stores. Check your local telephone directory. Sometimes when you purchase a computer it already has a word processing program installed.

PC vs. the Macintosh

There are several computer systems available for home computing but the two most common types of computers are the PC (personal computer), manufactured by companies such as DELL, IBM, NEC, GATEWAY, HP, SAMSUNG, and others — and the Macintosh manufactured by Apple Computer. The Macintosh computer is commonly referred to as a "Mac". Apple Computer has produced a PowerMac, an iMac, and a PowerMac G4, and the PowerMacG5. The operating system of the PowerMac G4 or G5 has undergone revisions.

Each major version also has a name: OS X version 10.2.x is Jaguar; version 10.3.x is Panther, and the version 10.4.x is Tiger. The Apple PowerMac computers(the G4 and the G5) have two processors (for parallel processing) instead of just one, and there is space inside the computer to upgrade to 4 hard disks in a RAID array to give more power to the computers functioning as a server. Sometimes the computer tower is called a "box" which is a slang word for "the computer". You could say, "there are two processors inside the box."

There is software specially designed for the PowerMac computers to help move files from a Windows 98, ME, or 2000 system (XP is not listed on the box) to the Mac OS X. This software is called Move2Mac and is a product of Detto Technologies. A lot of computer software can be purchased using a credit card with a secure connection over the Web, then downloading that software to your own computer. I prefer having a CD or other disk with the software on the disk.

Downloading via FTP is the process of moving files from another computer over a network connection to a local computer (like your own home computer) using File Transfer Protocol (FTP). If working at school or on the job you have to get permission to download files, for security reasons. You can download files using a Mac or a PC computer. Both use File Transfer Protocol.

The Macintosh has excelled in the commercial graphics and publishing industries and thousands of people prefer a Mac for home use rather than a PC. The PC computers currently have a much greater market share and there are millions in use in homes and businesses throughout the world. When you attend college the college will specify which type of computer, Mac or PC, will be in use at the college for faculty and students. Some colleges use just Mac computers in campus buildings and for the faculty. Other colleges use PCs.

Each PC running a specific operating system such as Windows 2000 is able to use any software that says WIN95/98/NT/2000 on the box. The Windows2000 operating system can also run any software specified for WIN95/98/NT/2000 as well as any software specified as Windows 9.x/NT/2000. If in doubt about buying the correct software for your system, the store clerks will be happy to assist you if asked. If you are using Windows XP, make sure that the software you buy has Windows XP included in the "System Requirements", usually found on the side panel of the box for shrink-wrapped software (boxed software).

Prior to the Macintosh OS X operating system the Macs used an operating system based upon a single processor (computer CPU) which processed data and ran applications using what was called cooperative multitasking. Cooperative multitasking allowed programs to sometimes take control of the central processing unit. Now with the newer Macintosh operating system, OS

10.2.x (Jaguar) and later versions there is a UNIX-like kernel in the operating system, two processors and the central processing unit processes data with symmetric multiprocessing and it uses preemptive multitasking, not allowing any application to take control of the central processing units.

If users want to run older software, the PowerMac G4 is a dual-booting machine meaning you can either boot into the older OS 9.2 or the newer OS X. (This is called "dual bootable".) Software written for the OS X (pronounced OS ten) will not run in the OS 9 environment but older legacy software is capable of being run while booted into the newer OS X, just that the newer features of the OS X will not be available when running applications designed for the OS 9 or older operating systems.

By contrast, the computer processor inside a PC or PC-clone computer has totally different architecture (microscopic "wiring" schematic) inside the central processing unit chip (the CPU, or "chip"). In other words, the specific way the circuits are laid out in a computer chip (CPU, central processing unit) is called the chip architecture. PC CPUs and Mac CPUs have chips with totally different architecture. Software is not interchangeable. Buy Mac software for the Macintosh and buy PC software for PC computers which use "486-type" architecture. An Apple or Mac computer is not a PC.

Most PC Computers are sold new with a Windows operating system but keep in mind that other operating systems can also run on PC-architecture machines. One example of another operating system that can run on a PC machine is Linux for Windows. When two operating systems are on a disk they are installed on separate "partitions" of the disk. That is similar to two songs on one CD having to be on separate "tracks". Usually, things you can see and touch on a computer or inside a computer are called "hardware" whereas programs for the computer (digital instructions) are called software.

Software is created by a computer programmer who writes lines of code for the computer. An interpreter or compiler is a smaller program which changes the programmer's code into machine instructions for the central processing unit. After much testing and debugging, the programmer's code is finally "packaged" into executable files which make up the final "software" which can be purchased later, or might be "bundled" with the computer when you buy it.

2

Computer Hardware

Everything you can see and touch in computer is hardware. The motherboard is the main circuit board in a PC. It contains all the circuits and components that run the PC. Major Components found on the motherboard are:

— *CPU*: the Central Processing Unit is often an Intel Pentium or Celeron processor. It is the heart of every PC. All scheduling, computation and control occurs here.

— *BIOS*: Basic Input Output System is a non-volatile memory that contains configuration information about the PC. It contains all the code required for the CPU to communicate with the keyboard, mouse video display, disk drives and communications devices. When a PC is powered on it uses the BIOS 'boot code' to set up many required functions that bring the PC to a point where it is ready to work.

— *RTC*: the Real Time Clock chip keeps date, day and time in a 24 hour format just like your watch. The PC uses this clock to 'time stamp' files as they are created and modified. When you print a file it time stamps the pages as they are printed.

— *Chip Set*: these are large chip(s) that integrate many functions that used to be found in separate smaller chips on the motherboard. They save space and cost.

The functions performed by these chip sets often broken into two devices with one providing an interface from the CPU to the memory and the other providing controllers for IDE, ISA, PCI and USB devices. Primary Connectors found on the motherboard are:

— Power: A 20 pin connector accepts a plug from the power supply. This plug carry DC power to all the circuits on the motherboard.

— Keyboard: A Mini-din 6-pin (round) connector found at the back of the motherboard is where the keyboard plugs in.

— Mouse: A Mini-din 6-pin connector found next to the keyboard connector is where the where the mouse plugs in.

— Display: This connector is not integrated into the motherboard but is included in this list since its function is absolutely necessary. It is a 15-pin, D-shell type connector found on a video card that plugs into the AGP connector of the motherboard.

— IDE: stands for Integrated Drive Electronics. These are 40 pin connectors that provide a place to connect the ribbon cables from the drives (hard and CD/DVD). All data between the motherboard and the drives is carried in these cables. They are not accessible unless the PC cover is removed.

— *FDD connector*: it is similar in function to the IDE connector. It is a 34 pin ribbon connector that carries data between the motherboard and any floppy drive installed in the PC. Not accessible with PC cover on.

— *DRAM*: Dynamic Random Access Memory connectors for SIMM and DIMM type memory modules. Not accessible with chassis cover on.

— *Serial Connectors*:

a) Standard Serial Connector: This connector has been around in PCs since they first appeared. It was originally located on ISA expansion type cards. Today it is an integral part of newer motherboards. It is a 9- pin, D-shell connector that allows you to connect external devices with serial ports to your PC. The maximum data rate is 115 KB/s.

b) *USB*: Universal Serial Bus This is a relatively new serial bus. Originally specified as low speed, 1.2 Mb/s, it was enhanced to full speed, 12Mb/s. The latest version 2.0 is specified as high speed, 400 MB/s. Someday USB will completely replace the standard serial connector that has been the workhorse serial port in earlier PCs. USB is now a standard connector on all new motherboards. Unlike serial and parallel ports, the USB port is designed to power devices connected to it. The devices must be low power devices and must be able to reduce their current draw to less than 0.5uAmps when commanded to do so by the PC.

— Parallel Connectors:

a) *Centronix or Standard Parallel*: This connector has been around in PCs since they first appeared. It has 37-pins and is now integrated on new motherboards. It is usually used to connect your printer to the PC and moves data at about 1MB/s.

b) *SCSI*: Small Computer System Interface moves data at a maximum of up to 80Mb/s. It not integrated into most PC motherboards. It can be added to a PC as an Expansion card. Some printers and hard disk drives use SCSI interfaces.

— *Expansion Card Connectors*: The CPU connects to expansion card connectors through one of the chip set ICs mentioned above. They are located on the motherboard near the rear of the PC. These connectors allow special function cards to plug into and work with the PC. Before motherboards integrated the serial and centronix connectors they were found on expansion boards that plugged into ISA slots. Most PCs have the following expansion connector types:

a) *ISA*: Industry Standard Architecture connectors have been around since 1980 and first appeared in the IBM XT PC. This type of slot still appears on some newer motherboards so that older expansion boards can still be used. However, many motherboards no longer have ISA connectors on them.

b) *PCI*: Peripheral Component Interconnect is a newer and faster interface that accepts all expansion cards that have a PCI interface.

c) *AGP*: Accelerated Graphics Port is a connector that is designed to work with video cards. Your video display plugs into and is controlled by one of these video cards. Many modern video cards offer enhanced 3D-graphics and fast, full motion video.

Power Supply

A power supply is installed in the back corner of the PC case, next to the motherboard. It converts 120vac (standard house power) into DC voltages that are used by other components in the PC. A 20 conductor cable carries +5vdc, -5vdc +12vdc, -12vdc and ground to the motherboard. Another pair of cables, each with four conductors and two 4-pin connectors daisy-chained along it, carry +5vdc, +12vdc and ground to the drives.

Hard Disk Drive

The HDD installs in one of the 3-1/2 inch internal drive

bays in the PC. It is secured by machine screws. It is powered by a 4 conductor cable coming from the power supply. Data to and from the motherboard is carried on a 40-pin IDE (Integrated Drive Electronics) cable. Data is stored magnetically on multiple rigid disks that are stacked up like pancakes. Small arms with magnetic pickups move rapidly back and forth across the top and bottom surface of each disk in the drive. The sensors float just a few microns above the rotating disk surface and can read and write data at very high rates. When one of these arms fails and nose dives into the disk surface a head crash occurs. This destroys a section of the disk surface and the data on it.

Specialists can take the drive apart and depending on where the crash occurred may be able to retrieve part of the information on the disks. Most commercially available hard drives rotate at 5400 or 7200 RPM (revolutions per minute) which translates to 90 or 120 revolutions per second respectively. The data transfer rate from the drive to the motherboard is measured in bursts of Mbytes/second. Newer drives are capable 133 Mbytes/ sec bursts. To use this faster drive, the PC must have an ATA/133 interface that is capable of keeping up with it.

Floppy Disk Drive

The FDD installs in one of the external drive bays at the front of the PC case and is secured by machine screws. External means you can access the drive from the outside. It is powered by a cable with a 4-pin connector that comes from the power supply. It transfers data to and from the motherboard by means of a 34 pin ribbon cable.

It stores data magnetically on a removable floppy disk. A pickup arm in the drive floats above the disk surface. The arm moves rapidly back and forth across the disk surface as a small magnetic sensor at the end of the arm reads and writes data on the rotating disk surface. Floppy disks hold 1.44 Mbytes, which at one time was a large amount of data. Today many programs and files are much larger than this. FDD are not offered in many PCs produced today. The PC case is a thin sheet metal enclosure that houses the motherboard, power supply and various drives (HDD, FDD, CD, DVD).

Cases are offered in two styles, desktop and tower. Today the tower type is predominant. It stands upright and is much taller than it is wide. It is usually placed on the floor next to, or under a desk. The desktop has a pizza box profile and usually sits on the desktop. Tower cases are offered in two basic sizes, one that can fit ATX (12" wide) motherboards and one that can accommodate ATX mini (8.5" wide) motherboards.

The number of drive bays offered also varies depending on manufacturer. The motherboard and power supply mount to the floor at the rear of the case. The drives (hard, floppy and CD/DVD) mount in enclosures called drive bays at the front of the case.

Compact Disk Drive

The CDD installs in one of the external 5-1/4 inch drive bays in the front of the PC case. It is secured by machine screws. Some manufacturers offer special rail-like systems that mount on the CDD. These allow the drive to be removed from the PC without having to remove any screws. Data is stored optically on the surface of the disk. A laser attached to an arm that moves back and forth across near the disk surface and sends light toward the disk surface which is coated with of a thin layer of aluminum.

Smooth areas called a lands reflect the light back to a photo diode located near the laser. The reflected light is read as a 1. Areas called pits are where the aluminum has been removed. When the laser light hits these, it is scattered and very little is picked up by the photo diode. The absence of light is read as a 0. CDD have become the predominant removable storage media for PCs and can store 700 Mbytes of data.

A 4-pin cable from the power supply plugs into the CDD and provides power to it. Data to and from the motherboard is carried on a 40-pin IDE (Integrated Drive Electronics) cable. There are two types of Compact Disk drives available for PCs.

a) CD-ROM (read only memory) is the older type. As the title implies it can only read CDs. It can read any standard CD and most CD-R type disks. It may be able to read some types of CD-RW disks too. A 24x CD-ROM unit costs about $30.

b) CD-RW (ReWritable)units can read and write CD-R and CD-RW type disks. It can also read standard CD type disks.

Digital Video Disk drive

DVD also known as the Digital Versatile Disk drive, installs in one of the external 5 1/4 inch drive bays in the PC. It is secured by machine screws. Some manufacturers offer special rail-like systems that mount on the DVD. These allow the drive to be removed from the PC without having to remove screws. It is designed to optically access data stored on a DVD. A laser moves back and forth near the disk surface and accesses data at a very fast rate. A 4-pin cable from the power supply plugs into the CDD and provides power to it. Data between the DVD drive and the motherboard is carried on a 40-pin IDE (Integrated Drive Electronics) cable. There are two types of DVD drives that typically go into PCs.

a) DVD-ROM (Read Only Memory) can read DVDs and CDs and costs about $75.

b) DVD-RAM (Random Access Memory) units can read and write DVDs.

A standard DVD stores up to 4.7 Gbytes on one side of the disk. Digitally formatted movies can be stored on a standard DVD in MPEG-2 format.

Monitor

CRT Monitors

Up until recently, CRTs (Cathode RayTubes) were the only type of displays for use with desktop PCs. They are relatively big (14" to 16" deep) and heavy (over 15 lbs). They are available in screen sizes from 14" to 21". A 17" display means that it is 17" measured diagonally from one corner of the tube to the other. The actual viewing area is smaller than 17" (about 16") since the electron gun can't sweep completely to the tube edge. CRTs send a stream of electrons at the screen, which is charged to about 25,000 volts. As they strike it they cause phosphor on the backside of the screen to glow creating light which you see.

The electron stream is sweep back and forth and up and down at about 60 sweeps per second and turned off and on at the right time to make text and graphics images appear. They are powered by standard 120Vac wall power. Data is transferred to the display on a cable with a 15-pin D-shell connector that plugs into a connector on the video card which in turn plugs into one of the PC's expansion slots.

LCD Monitors

Liquid Crystal Display (LCD) technology has been used in laptops for some time. It has recently been made commercially available as monitors for desktop PCs. LCDs have no electron gun and are therefore not very deep like CRTs. The text and images you see are created by a back light behind the panel, that shines through pixels (picture elements). Each pixel is made up of three chambers red, green and blue. The chambers in each pixel must be opened enough and in the proper proportion to produce the correct brightness and color.

In TFT (Thin Film Transistor) type LCDs, each pixel is controlled by a tiny transistor that opens and closes the chambers in each pixel. Desk top LCD displays are powered by standard 120Vac wall power. Data is transferred to the display on a cable with a 15-pin connector that plugs into a mating connector on the video card seated in an expansion slot in the PC.

Keyboard

The keyboard was the first input device developed for the PC. The standard keyboard layout provides 104 keys organized as four groups:

a) alphanumeric keys (A-Z, 0-9)

b) location keys (home, end etc.)

c) numeric keypad

d) function keys (F1-F12)

In addition to the standard keys, some keyboards offer functions such as volume control for speakers, web browser functions and power management. Data is transferred to the PC over a short cable with a circular 6-pin Mini-din connector that plugs into the back of the motherboard. There are wireless keyboards that communicate with a pod that is plugged into the keyboard port. Radio Frequency (RF) or InfraRed (IR) technology is used to communicate between the keyboard and the receiver pod, which plugs into the PC. Cherry Hill Inc. is releasing a keyboard that has an integrated Finger Tip sensor. Instead of having to type in passwords to access the PC a successful fingerprint match allows entry in to the PC or specific programs.

Mouse

The mouse is the most common 'pointing device' used in PCs. Every mouse has two buttons and most have one or two scroll wheels. By default the left button is used to select items. The right button is assigned as a context or alternate menu. A single wheel is normally set to scroll up and down on the active page. If a second wheel is present, it is usually assigned to scroll left and right on the page. The button functions can be reassigned by going to Control Panel > Mouse > Buttons tab.

Data is transferred to the PC over a short cable with a circular 6-pin Mini-din connector that plugs into the back of the motherboard. This type of mouse sells for $10 to $25 depending on the style, button and wheel configuration. Some versions of the mouse are wireless. They communicate with a receiver pod that is plugs into the mouse port. Radio Frequency (RF) or InfraRed (IR) technology is used for communication between the mouse and the pod. These sell in the $30 to $45 range. There are two designs used in a mouse for detecting motion:

Track ball: This type of mouse uses a rolling (track) ball. As the mouse moves the ball rolls. The rolling motion is converted electronically into matching movements of the mouse pointer that moves across your video display. The track ball mouse is rapidly becoming another casualty of rapidly changing technology. The optical mouse has pretty much replaced it. The track ball mouse is already becoming a thing of the past.

Optical: This mouse uses an InfraRed transmitter/ receiver pair to optically detect the motion of the mouse. It has a number of advantages over the track ball mouse:

— No mouse pad is required.

— Can work on any flat surface

— No rolling track ball that collects and transfers dirt to the internal rollers, making them slip. When they do, your mouse pointer jumps around in an unpredictable and annoying way!

Audio

Speakers and headphones are the primary audio output devices for a PC. Some monitors have speakers hn Anthony built into their sides. Other speakers are free standing. Passive speakers plug into and are powered directly from the output signal provided by the 'speaker out' port on the sound card. Active speakers amplify the sound signal from the sound card using battery or rectified AC house power

Cables and Wires

Although these are not the most sophisticated part of the system, they are just as important as any other component. All the components in a PC are connected together and to power with wires and cables.

3

Computer Software

The software is the information that the computer uses to get the job done. Software needs to be accessed before it can be used. There are many terms used for process of accessing software including running, executing, starting up, opening, and others. Computer programs allow users to complete tasks. A program can also be referred to as an application and the two words are used interchangeably. Examples of software programs or applications would be the Operating System (DOS, Windows 9x/Millenium/XP, O/S2, UNIX, MacOS 9.x/10.x and various others), Wordprocessor (typing letters), Spreadsheet (financial info), Database (inventory control and address book), Graphics program, Internet Browser, Email and many others.

As well any document that you create, graphic you design, sound you compose, file you make, letter you write, email you send or anything that you create on your computer is referred to as software. All software is stored in files. Software is stored on a disk or tape whether that disk is a floppy, hard disk, CD, tape or one of the dozens of other storage devices available. There are millions of different pieces of software available for almost every conceivable need. Software is available commercially through stores and mail order and also available on the Internet.

Software is also available through an Open Source license which allows anyone to use the Open Source software free of charge as long as the license is maintained. If you can't find the application that you need software development companies can custom design software for you. The largest software companies offer packages of software or suites that include many of the programs that the average person or business needs. Software packages or suites contain programs that work together and share information, making it easier to combine that information in versatile ways.

For example when writing a letter you can get the mailing address from an address book, include a letterhead from a graphics program and included a financial chart from a spreadsheet and combine this collection of information in the body of the letter. The three basic types of software are; commercial, shareware and open source software. Some software is also release into the public domain without a license.

Commercial software comes prepackaged and is available from software stores and through the Internet.

Shareware is software developed by individual and small companies that cannot afford to market their software world wide or by a company that wants to release a demonstration version of their commercial product. You will have an evaluation period in which you can decide whether to purchase the product or not. Shareware software often is disabled in some way and has a notice attached to explain the legal requirements for using the product.

Open Source software is created by generous programmers and released into the public domain for public use. There is usually a copyright notice that must remain with the software product. Open Source software is not public domain in that the company or individual that develops the software retains ownership of the program but the software can be used freely. Many popular Open Source applications are being developed and upgraded regularly by individuals and companies that believe in the Open Source concept.

Operating Systems (OS)

All computers need some sort of Operating System. The majority of modern home computers use some form of Microsoft's operating systems. The original Microsoft operating system was called DOS (Disk Operating System) though most computers use Windows. Windows comes in various versions beginning with version 3.x then 95, 98, ME and currently XP. A few computers use IBM's O/S2. Apple's Mac use their own operating system beginning with OS 1 though most modern Macs use version 8.x or 9.x. Apple's latest version is OS 10.1.x.

In the past large companies and institutions would have an operating system design exclusively for them but as the commercial operating systems become more sophisticated the benefits of this practice is becoming less apparent. Some computer professionals, Internet Service Providers (ISP) and mainframe computer users use an operating system such as UNIX (or a variant such as Linux), Windows NT or 2000 (Win2k) or one of the other network or server based operating systems.

There are many smaller operating systems out there. The problem is that software is currently being developed only for the main operating systems and only the newest versions of these OS. Many older computers with unique operating systems have lots of software already developed for them but there is very little new software being developed for the older computers. The older proprietary operating systems are less likely to offer technical support than the more modern operating systems. The operating system controls the input and output or directs the flow of information to and from the CPU. Much of this is done automatically by the system but it is possible to modify and control your system if you need to.

When you turn your computer on it first needs to load the operating system sometimes referred to a booting up. Basically the computer starts from scratch every time you turn the power on. It checks all its components and will usually display a message if there is a problem. Loading the system is usually automatic. Once the system is loaded the user can start the application or program that they are going to use. Most computer users will run Microsoft Windows, Mac OS or Linux as their operating system. These OS are Graphic User Interface (GUI) which allows the user to control or run the computer using a Mouse and Icons.

The user simply moves the mouse on a flat surface, rolls the trackball, or moves their hand over the touchpad to control a pointer. They then choose the option they want by pressing a button or touching the pad. Without a GUI the user controls the computer using the keys on the keyboard. This is referred to as a Command Line Interface (CLI)

Disk and Storage

Disks are used to store information. All information on computers are stored in files. The size of a file is measured in bytes. A byte is approximately one character (letter 'a', number '1', symbol '?' etc....).

— About a thousand bytes is a kilobyte (KB).

— About a million bytes is a megabyte (MB).

— About a billion bytes is a gigabyte (GB).

A byte is made up of 8 bits. A bit is simply an on or an off signal which passes through the computers circuitry.

Every piece of software can be broken down into a series of on or off signals or it's Binary Code.

Floppy disk are still a common way of transporting information (such as bringing files home from work) but compact disks (CDs) and Digital Video Devices (DVDs) are becoming more popular. Most software is sold on a CD. Hard disks are the most common storage device. Compact disks or CDs can store large amounts of information. One disk will store 650 Mb or about 70 or 80 minutes of music.

One type is a CD-ROM which stand for Compact Disk Read Only Memory. Another type is a CD-RW which stands for Compact Disk - Read/Write. CD drives can copy information or burn information on to a blank CD. Common Read Only CD blanks can only be written to once though more expensive Read/Write CD's can be used over and over again. DVD disks can store over 4 gigabytes. DVD recorders allow you to store large files, such as movies, on a single disk.

Hard disks store the majority of information on today's modern computer. My first hard disk stored 52 Mb, 12 more than my colleague's 40 Mb. Today the standard hard disk stores 30 GB or more (this number is constantly increasing). Like a floppy disk information can be stored and deleted as necessary. As files get larger the speed that hard disks can read and write become more important. Floppy disk or diskette comes in two basic sizes; 5.25 inch (almost obsolete) and 3.5 inch. Both have a low and high density versions though 3.5 inch high density disks are the most common.

There are many other storage devices including tapes, Panasonic's LS120 3.5 inch diskettes, Iomega's Zip & Jazz disks, VCR tape and many others. Innovation in storage technology is currently advancing rapidly. Information is stored in an electromagnetic form much like a cassette or video tape.

4

Personel Computers

The term personal computer or PC is generally a microcomputer intended to be used by one person at a time, and suitable for general purpose tasks such as word processing, programming, or game play, usually used to run purchased or other software not written by the user. Unlike minicomputers, a personal computer is often owned by the person using it, indicating a low cost of purchase and simplicity of operation. The user of a modern personal computer may have significant knowledge of the operating environment and application programs, but is not necessarily interested in programming nor even able to write programs for the computer.

The first generation of microcomputers were called just that, and only sold in small numbers to those able to (build them from kits or) operate them: engineers and accomplished hobbyists (for example, the Altair 8800). The second generation micros were known as home computers. The earliest known use of the term was in New Scientist magazine in 1964, in a series of articles called "The World in 1984". In "The Banishment of Paper Work," Arthur L. Samuel of IBM's Watson Research Center writes, "While it will be entirely feasible to obtain an education at home, via one's own personal computer, human nature will not have changed."

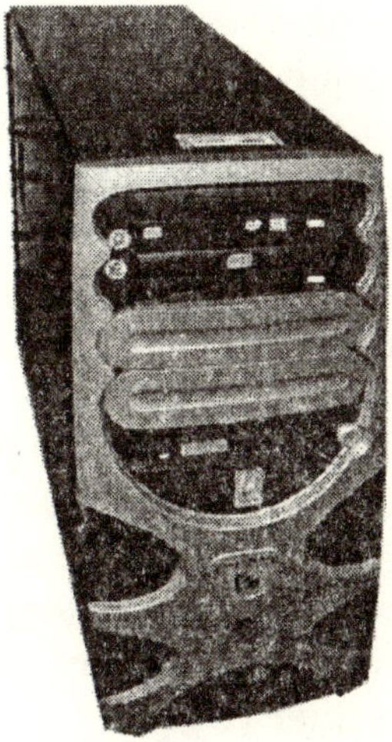

The tower of a personal computer.

The first computers that can be called 'personal' were the first non-mainframe computers, the LINC and the PDP-8. By today's standards they were big (about the size of a refrigerator), expensive (around $50,000 US), and had small magnetic core memories (about 4096 12-bit words for the LINC).

However, they were small enough and cheap enough for individual laboratories and research projects to use, freeing them from the batch processing and bureaucracy of the typical industrial or university computing center. In addition, they were moderately interactive and soon had their own operating systems. Eventually, this category became known as the mini-computer, usually with time-sharing and program development facilities. Eventually, the mini-computer grew up to encompass the VAX and larger mini-computers from Data General, Prime, and others. Deployment of mini-computer systems was a model for how personal computers would be used, but few of the mini-computer makers managed to profit from it.

Development of the single-chip microprocessor changed everything, since it dropped the cost of purchase of a computer by an order of magnitude or more. The first generation of microcomputers that started to appear in the mid 1970s were less powerful and in some ways less versatile than business computers of the day (but in other ways more versatile, in terms of built-in sound and graphics capabilities), and were generally used by computer enthusiasts for learning to program, for running simple office/productivity applications, for electronics interfacing, and/or games, as well as for accessing BBS's, general online services such as CompuServe, The Source, or Genie, or platform-specific services such as Quantum Link (US) or Compunet (UK).

Personal computer and peripherals. From left to right: ink jet printer, an irrelevant TV, CRT monitor, broadband cable modem for the internet, flat bed scanner. The tower (CPU, hard drive, etc) can just be glimpsed at bottom right. The keyboard and mouse are wireless.

It was the launch of the VisiCalc spreadsheet, initially for the Apple II and later for the Atari 8-bit family, Commodore PET, and IBM PC that became the "killer app" that turned the microcomputer into a business tool. Later, Lotus 1-2-3, a combined spreadsheet (partly based on VisiCalc), presentation graphics, and simple database application, became the PCs own killer app. Good word processor programs also appeared for many home computers. The low cost of personal computers led to great popularity in the home and business markets during the 1980s.

A Micron TransPort XPE laptop computer.

During the 1990s, the power of personal computers increased radically, blurring the formerly sharp distinction between personal computers and multi-user computers such as mainframes. Today higher-end computers often distinguish themselves from personal computers by greater reliability or greater ability to multitask, rather than by straight CPU power.

Personal computers can be categorized by size and portability:

— the desktop computer

— the portable computer

— the notebook or laptop

— the tablet computer

— the PDA

— the wearable computer

Many mass-market IBM PC compatible and Apple Macintosh personal computers are standardized to the point that purchased software is expected to run with little or no customization for the particular computer. Often memory, and peripherals such as video boards and disk storage are easily upgradable, even by the end user, and even the motherboard can in some cases be changed to upgrade the power of the central processor.

Such upgradeability is not indefinite since major changes in the personal computer industry occur every three to five years; a machine that was considered top-of-the-line say five or six years ago may be impractical to upgrade due to changes in processors, memory, and peripherals. This upgrade cycle is in part linked to new releases of the primary mass-market operating system, which tends to drive the accquisition of new hardware and tends to obsolete previously serviceable hardware.

The hardware capabilities of personal computers can sometimes be extended by the addition of expansion cards. The standard expansion bays for personal computers as of 2005 are ISA, PCI and AGP. A PC may also be upgraded by the addition of extra drives (DVD, CD-ROM, flash drive, Hard drive, etc). Standard storage device interfaces are ATA, Serial ATA or SCSI in 2005.

Motherboard

The motherboard is the primary circuit board for a computer. Most other computer components plug directly into the motherboard to allow them to exchange information. Motherboards usually hold a chipset, BIOS, CMOS (PC), parallel port, PS/2 keyboard and mouse ports and expansion bays. Sometimes a secondary daughter board is plugged into the motherboard to provide more expansion bays and to cut down on its size.

Central Processing Unit (CPU)

The Central processing unit or CPU is the part of the computer that performs most of the calculations that make programs or operating systems run. The CPU plugs directly into the motherboard by one of many different types of sockets. Most IBM PC compatible computers use an x86-compatible processor made by Intel, AMD, VIA Technologies or Transmeta.

Random Access Memory (RAM)

The Random Access Memory of the computer is the "short-term-memory" of the PC, It is much faster than the mass storage devices like Harddisk or CD-ROM, but its contents are lost when the Power is turned off.

IBM PC

Though many personal computers are IBM PC compatible using either Microsoft Windows or open-source forms of UNIX such as Linux, a number of other personal computer types are still popular. The leading alternative is Apple Computer's Power Macintosh platform, based on the PowerPC microprocessor. Further PC and PW (Personal Workstation) types through time:

- Acorn Archimedes & RiscPC
- Atari ST
- BeOS BeBox
- Amiga
- Pegasos
- NEC PC-9800 (At one time, in Japan)
- NeXT workstations
- Sun SparcStation
- SGI workstations like the SGI Indigo and SGI Onyx

The term "personal computer" is often avoided by advocates of the above computer systems, ostensibly because of the association it has to the "PC" in "IBM PC".

5

Microsoft Windows

Microsoft Windows is a range of operating environments for personal computers and servers. The range was first introduced by Microsoft in 1985 and eventually has come to dominate the world personal computer market. All recent versions of Windows are fully-fledged operating systems. Windows is proprietary closed source software: Microsoft Corporation owns the software's copyright and controls its distribution.

Windows was developed for IBM PC-compatible computers (these were based on Intel x86 architecture), and today, almost all versions of Windows are made for this hardware-platform (although Windows NT was written as a cross-platform system for Intel and MIPS processors, and later appeared on the PowerPC and DEC Alpha architectures). The popularity of Windows made Intel CPUs more popular and vice versa. In fact, the term Wintel became used to describe PC-compatible computers running a version of Windows.

The term Windows is used as a collective term for several generations of products, which can be classified into the following categories:

16-bit operating environments: Although they are often thought of as just graphical user interfaces or desktops, mostly because they use MS-DOS for file system services,

16-bit Windows versions already have their own executable file format and provide their own device drivers (graphics, printer, mouse, keyboard and sound). Most importantly, from the beginning they allow the user to (non-preemptively) multi-task graphical applications, something which competitors like GEM do not offer.

Finally, they implement an elaborated segment-based software virtual memory scheme, which allows to run applications larger than available memory: code segments and resources are swapped in and thrown away when useless or memory becomes scarce and data segments move in memory when a given application has relinquished processor control. Examples include Windows 1.0 and Windows 2.0 and its close relative Windows/286.

Hybrid 16/32-bit operating environments: Windows/386 introduced a 32-bit protected mode kernel and virtual machine monitor. For the duration of a Windows session, it provided a device virtualization for the disk controller, video card, keyboard, mouse, timer and interrupt controller. The user-visible consequence was that it became possible to preemptively multitask multiple MS-DOS environments in separate windows (graphical applications required switching the window to full screen mode). Windows applications were still multi-tasked cooperatively inside one of such real-mode environments.

Windows 3.0 (1990) and Windows 3.1 (1992) perfected the design, notably thanks to virtual memory and loadable virtual device drivers (VxDs) which allowed them to share arbitrary devices between multitasked DOS windows. Most important, Windows applications could now run in 16-bit protected mode (when Windows was running in Standard or 386 Enhanced Mode), which gave them access to several megabytes of memory and removed the obligation to participate in the software virtual memory scheme. They still ran inside the same address space, where the segmented memory provided a degree of protection, and multi-tasked cooperatively. For Windows 3.0 Microsoft also rewrote critical operations from C into assembly, making this release faster and less memory-hungry than its predecessors.

Hybrid 16/32-bit operating system: With the introduction of 32-Bit File Access in Windows for Workgroups 3.11, Windows could finally stop relying on DOS for file management. Leveraging this, Windows 95 introduced Long File Names, reducing the 8.3 DOS to the role of a boot loader. MS-DOS was now bundled with Windows; this notably made it (partially) aware of long file names when its utilities were run from within Windows, but angered the competition. The most important novelty was however the possibility of running 32-bit multi-threaded preemptively multitasked graphical programs.

There were three releases of Windows 95 (the first in 1995, then subsequent bug-fix versions in 1996 and 1997, only released to OEMs, which added extra features such as FAT32 support). Microsoft's next OS was Windows 98; there were two versions of this. This was an evolutionary enhancement, in much the same relation to Windows 98 as Windows 3.1 had been to 3.0. In 2000, Microsoft released Windows Me, which used the same core as Windows 98 but adopted the visual appearance of Windows 2000, as well as a new feature called system restore, allowing the user to set the computer's settings back to an earlier date. Compared to previous upgrades, comparatively few people bothered to switch to ME: by this time most power users had already jumped over to the NT family. This can be defended by the fact that Microsoft left little time for Windows Millennium to become popular before announcing their next version of Windows.

32-bit operating systems originally designed and marketed for higher-reliability business use with no DOS heritage. The first release was Windows NT 3.1 (1993, numbered "3.1" to match the Windows version and to 1-

up OS/2 2.1, its main competitor at the time), which was followed by NT 3.5 (1994), NT 3.51 (1995), and NT 4.0 (1996); the latter of which introduced the Windows 95 interface. Microsoft then moved to combine their consumer and business operating systems. Their first attempt, Windows 2000, failed to meet their goals, and was released as a business system. The home consumer edition of Windows 2000, codenamed "Windows Neptune", ceased development and Microsoft released Windows ME in its place.

Eventually "Neptune" was merged into their new project, Whistler, which later became Windows XP. XP finally rendered DOS obsolete, and since then a new business system, Windows Server 2003, has expanded the top end of the range, and the forthcoming Windows Longhorn will complete it. Windows CE, Microsoft's offering in the mobile and embedded markets, is also a true 32-bit operating system.

64-bit operating systems, the newest category, are designed for AMD's AMD64 CPU architecture, Intel's Intel Architecture 64-bit, and EM64T. The 64-bit Windows family comprises Windows XP Itanium edition, Professional x64 Edition, and Windows Server 2003; Windows XP Professional and Server 2003 x64 editions were released on April 25, 2005. Itanium editions already came out in 2002. Early indications are that Windows Longhorn, the projected successor to Windows XP, will be released in both 32-Bit and 64-Bit versions.

Interface

The most obvious feature of the more recent Windows versions (since Windows 95 and NT 4.0) is the desktop, which is similar to the "Workplace Shell" introduced by IBM for OS/2 2.0 in 1992, an object-oriented GUI running on the OS/2 Presentation Manager. The Windows desktop has produced a significant change in the way people and computers interact; it is possible to perform many common tasks with very little computer knowledge, including some quite complex ones.

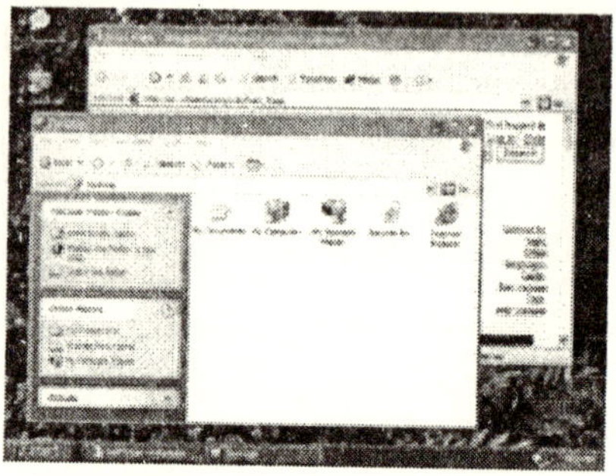

A typical Windows XP desktop.

Another quite significant feature of Windows since Windows 95 is the Start Button and Start Menu, which gives users of any skill level immediate access to all of their installed programs, and many of the other features of the operating system. Windows XP introduced a new visual style dubbed "Luna", which updated the classic Windows style (a plain grey box look) with a more graphical appearance. The new style features bold colors and a larger titlebar and start button, leading many to call it the "playskool" interface (after a popular brand of children's toys) and others to call it the "Teletubbies" interface (after the children TV show Teletubbies, also partly because of Windows XP's default wallpaper, a grassy plain with a blue sky, which resembles the set of the TV show).

Users can still elect to use the old Windows 95/2000 visual style. There is a view that modern operating systems need to cater to the vastly increased user base with a lower average computer skill level and the increased power and complexity of modern computer systems. Therefore, some technically savvy users accuse the Windows interface of isolating the user from too much of the inner workings of the computer, making it more difficult to control and configure some system features, although many such features can be now controlled also from the command-line or by scripting. However, this has always been an issue to some extent with GUI operating systems, and, to a lesser extent, almost all operating systems, by definition.

Thought to be installed on over 90% of personal computers, Windows has achieved enormous market penetration due in large part to the domination of MS-DOS in the early days of PC compatible computers (IBM-PC clones), and also because it is the primary platform for Microsoft Office and gaming software programs used by many microcomputer users. Although some of these factors have faded over the years (such as the sunset of the MS-DOS, the ability of third-party software like Open Office to create and/or modify Microsoft Office documents, or the porting of notable games to Macintosh and Linux), these factors helped create a dedicated early userbase.

Microsoft's operating system has also benefited from the fact that they are one of the few companies that are willing to license their OSes to hardware manufacturers. (For example, Apple is loath to license Mac OS X and Sun does not license Solaris to anyone.) Before, companies who wanted to be in the computer business had to create their own operating system (such as the Amiga) or use a OS without a GUI (like MS-DOS or CP/M); even an exclusive license was significantly cheaper than developing a new operating system and creating a software base. Thus, Microsoft won much early support.

Due to Microsoft's exclusive licensing agreements with many computer vendors, Windows today comes pre-installed on most computers as a bundled OEM version, making it the default choice for much of the market. Most consumers do not delete Windows and install another operating system. For some consumers, Windows is the only valid option as their computing environment is mandated by their workplace; additionally, the unfamiliarity of most other operating systems limits the desire to switch to other operating systems. Additionally, a growing part of the computer market (the "AOL generation") lacks the technical knowledge needed to install an operating system.

Finally, the software base of programs available for the Windows family of operating systems (generally greater than that of all other operating systems combined) has become the single largest self-perpetuating reason for the popularity of Windows. In recent years, many companies have started up with the sole intention of releasing Windows software; the fact that there is already a large customer base in place is reason enough for such companies to only spend resources on Windows software development. In turn, the fact that many companies are supporting Windows exclusively is reason for many customers to choose Windows.

Security

Security has been a major weakness of Windows for many years. Most modern operating systems were designed for security in a multi-user and/or networked environment and have a relatively small number of security issues. Windows was originally designed for ease-of-use on a single-user PC without a network connection, and did not have security features built in from the outset. Combined with occasionally flawed code (such as buffer overruns) Windows has been the successful target of worms and virus writers numerous times.

Some say Microsoft Windows gets more than its fair share of attacks simply because it is the dominant desktop operating system. Others say it gets more attacks because poor engineering design makes it such an easy target: its monolithic and entangled structure is in stark contrast to the rigorous modularity and carefully defined layers of its rivals. Microsoft publicly admitted their ongoing security problems shortly after the turn of the century and (according to their press statements) now claims to regard security as their number one priority.

Microsoft releases security patches through its Windows Update service approximately once a month, although critical updates are made available at shorter intervals. In Windows 2000 and Windows XP, updates can be automatically downloaded and installed if the user elects to do so. Many security experts are advising Windows users to take steps to increase the security of their systems.

Much documentation is available describing how to increase the security of Microsoft Windows products. Typical suggestions include deploying Microsoft Windows behind a hardware firewall, running anti-virus and anti-spyware software, and installing patches as they become available through Windows Update. Some suggest replacing specific programs which are often targeted by crackers with alternatives, such as replacing the web browser Internet Explorer with Mozilla Firefox, and replacing the email client Microsoft Outlook with Mozilla Thunderbird.

In 2001, Microsoft started talking about a controversial security initiative called Palladium. The system has since been renamed "Next Generation Secure Computing Base". Palladium is a system intended to allow a program to verify that it is unmodified, and is running on "trusted" hardware with "trusted" drivers and a "trusted" architecture. This, in theory, assures the software that it is running on unmodified software and hardware. Palladium has a particular use in DRM systems. A side effect will be to lock out "untrusted" operating systems at the hardware level: this is likely to impact Linux in particular, since there is no single canonical Linux which can be certified, and many users consider the ability to customize the system one of its main attractions.

Some conspiracy theorists hold that this is the secret reason behind the system, although in practice it is unlikely that Microsoft will try to prevent Linux vendors such as Red Hat from having their products certified. As of 2004, Palladium has not resulted in any commercial products.

Current versions

— Windows CE for embedded systems including Consumer Electronics products

— Windows Mobile for smart phones and PDAs (a version of Windows CE)

  a) Portable Media Center for Digital Media Players

— Windows XP for desktops and laptops (notebooks)

  a) Windows XP Starter Edition, for new computer users in developing countries

  b) Windows XP Home Edition, for home desktops and laptops

  c) Windows XP Home Edition N, as above, but without a default installation of Windows Media Player, as mandated by an EU ruling

  d) Windows XP Professional Edition, for business and power users

  e) Windows XP Professional Edition N, as above, but without a default installation of Windows Media Player, as mandated by an EU ruling

f) Windows XP Professional x64 Edition, for PC's with 64-bit processors (based on Windows Server 2003)

g) Windows XP Tablet PC Edition, for notebooks with a touch screen or a pen-sensitive screen

h) Windows XP Media Center Edition for desktops and notebooks with an emphasis on audio, video, and PVR capability

— Windows Server 2003 for servers

a) Small Business Server for first server installations (up to 2 processors)

b) Web Edition for basic web serving (up to 2 processors)

c) Standard Edition for smaller server applications that don't require clustering (up to 4 processors)

d) Enterprise Edition for larger server applications, and clustering (up to 8 processors)

e) Datacenter Edition for mainframe like servers (up to 128 processors)

f) Storage Server for Network Attached Storage Devices

— Windows XP Embedded for embedded systems

Past Versions

— DOS-Based

a) 1985 November - Windows 1.0

b) 1987 December 9 - Windows 2.0

c) 1990 May 22 - Windows 3.0

d) 1992 August - Windows 3.1

e) 1992 October - Windows for Workgroups 3.1

f) 1993 November - Windows for Workgroups 3.11

g) 1995 August 24 - Windows 95 (Version number: 4.00.950)

h) 1998 June 25 - Windows 98 (Version number: 4.1.1998)

i) 1999 May 5 - Windows 98 Second Edition (Version number: 4.1.2222)

j) 2000 June 19 - Windows Me (Version number; 4.9.3000)

— NT Kernel-Based

a) 1993 August - Windows NT 3.1

b) 1994 September - Windows NT 3.5

c) 1995 June - Windows NT 3.51

d) 1996 July 29 - Windows NT 4.0 - the last version which ran on RISC architectures like DEC Alpha, MIPS and PowerPC. Later versions concentrated on x86-based hardware and - mainly as server OSs - the IA-64 line of CPUs.

e) 2000 February 17 - Windows 2000 (Version number: NT 5.0.2195)

Future Versions

— 2006 - Windows codename "Longhorn" is scheduled to be released.

— 2010-2012 - Windows codename "Blackcomb".

— Windows Eiger - is in early development, designed for old machines.

Emulation and virtual Machine Software

Emulation or the use of "virtual machines" allow the use of some Windows applications without using Microsoft Windows.

— WINE is an incomplete open source implementation of the Windows API, allowing one to run some Windows applications on x86 Unix-based platforms, including Linux.

— Cedega (formerly known as WineX) is TransGaming Technologies' proprietary fork of WINE, which is designed specifically for running games written for Microsoft Windows under Linux

— Java programming language by Sun Microsystems - Java is an object-oriented programming language developed initially by James Gosling and colleagues at Sun Microsystems.

— Microsoft.NET Web Application Platform

— ReactOS - Open Source operating system, aimed to be compatible with Windows NT apps and drivers, although still very much in its infancy at the moment.

— Freedows and Alliance OS - A very ambitious project, and a subsequent spinoff, that tried to clone Windows but withered away.

— Project David - Ambitious and controversial project to fully emulate Windows programs to run on other OSs.

— Codeweavers CrossOver Office product, also to fully emulate Windows programs to run on other OSs.

— VMWare PC Emulator software

— Microsoft Virtual PC (formerly by Connectix)

— Captive NTFS - A software "wrapper" for fuller, more-compatible open-source implementations of the Windows NTFS file system

- QEMU - Free software written by Fabrice Bellard that implements a fast processor emulator, allowing a user to run one operating system within another
- DOSBox - An emulator which creates a DOS-like environment primarily intended for running older, MS-DOS-based PC computer games which may not run properly on newer PCs.
- ScummVM - A virtual machine which allows one to play LucasArts Adventure Games games which use the SCUMM system on platforms other than those where versions were originally released.
- E/OS - Goal to make it possible to run any program designed for any operating system without the need to actually install any other operating system

6

Microsoft Word

Microsoft Word is a word processor program from Microsoft. It was originally written by Richard Brodie for IBM PC computers running DOS in 1983. Later versions were created for the Apple Macintosh, SCO UNIX, and Microsoft Windows. It became part of the Microsoft Office.

Word's first general release was for MS-DOS computers in late 1983. It was not well received, and sales lagged behind those of rival products such as WordPerfect. On the Macintosh, however, Word gained wide acceptance after it was released in 1985, and especially with the second major release, Word 3.01 for Macintosh, two years later (Word 3.00 was plagued with bugs and quickly superseded). Like other Mac software, Word for Mac was a true what-you-see-is-what-you-get (WYSIWYG) editor.

Although MS-DOS was a character-based system, Word for DOS was the first word processor for the IBM PC that showed typeface markups such as bold and italics directly on the screen while editing, although this was not a true WYSIWYG system. Other DOS word processors, such as WordStar and WordPerfect, used simple text-only display with markup codes on the screen or sometimes, at the most, alternative colors.

However, as with most DOS software, each program had its own, often complicated, set of commands for performing functions that had to be learned (for example, in Word for DOS, a file would be saved with the sequence Escape-T-S), and as most secretaries had learned how to use WordPerfect, companies were reluctant to switch to a rival product that offered few advantages.

Microsoft Word 6.0 (Windows 98)

The first version of Word for Windows was released in 1989 at a price of 500 US dollars. With the release of Windows 3.0 the following year, sales began to pick up (Word 1.0 worked much better with Windows 3.0 than with previous versions). The failure of WordPerfect to produce a Windows version proved a fatal mistake. It was version 2.0 of Word, however, that firmly established Microsoft Word as the market leader.

Word on the Macintosh never had any serious rivals, although programs such as Nisus Writer provided features such as non-contiguous selection which were not added until Word 2002 in Office XP. In addition, some users complained that Word had not had a major overhaul between versions 3.01 in 1987 and version 5.0 in 1991. Word 5.1 for the Macintosh was a popular word processor due to its elegance, relative ease of use, and feature set. However, version 6.0 for the Macintosh, released 1994, was widely derided. It was the first version of Word based on a common codebase between the Windows and Mac versions; many accused it of being slow, clumsy and memory intensive.

The Windows version was also numbered 6.0 to coordinate product naming across platforms. Later versions of Word have more capabilities than just word processing. The Drawing tool allows simple desktop publishing operations such as adding graphics to documents. Collaboration, document comparison, multilingual support and many other capabilities have been added over the years.

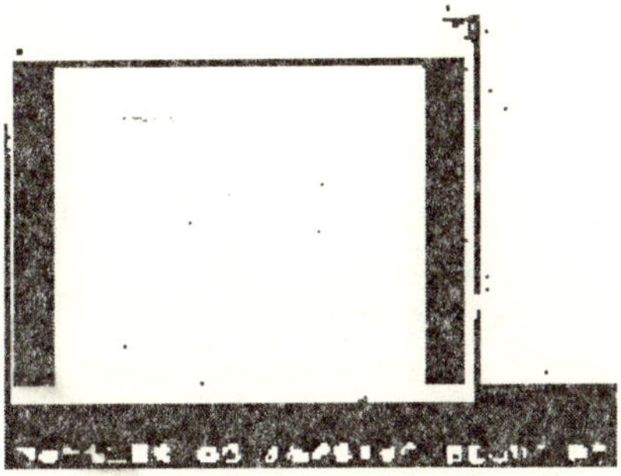

Microsoft Word X (Mac OS X)

Microsoft Word is the dominant word processor in current use, making Word's proprietary document file format (DOC) the de facto standard which competing products must support to interoperate in an office environment. File import and export filters exist for many word processors such as AbiWord or OpenOffice.org. Most of this interoperability is achieved through reverse engineering since documentation of the file format, while available to partners, is not openly available. The document formats of the various versions of Word change in subtle and not so subtle ways; formatting created in newer versions does not always survive when viewed in older versions of the program, nearly always because that capability does not exist in the previous version.

The DOC format of Word 97 was publicly documented by Microsoft, but later versions have been kept private, available only to partners, governments and institutions. Industry rumors claim some aspects of the Word file format are at present not fully understood even by Microsoft themselves. Lately Microsoft has stated that they will move towards an XML-based file format for their office applications. Word 2003 has an XML file format as an option using a publicly documented schema called

WordprocessingML, endorsed by such institutions as the Danish Government. The "professional" edition includes the ability to handle non-Microsoft schemas directly in Word. Apache Jakarta POI is an open-source Java library that aims to read and write Word's binary file format.

Like other Microsoft Office applications, Word can be highly customised using a built-in macro language (originally WordBasic, but changed to Visual Basic for Applications as of Word 97). However, this capability can also be used to embed viruses in documents, as was demonstrated by the Melissa worm. This is just another reason why computer users should have a firewall and anti-virus software installed on their system and follow Microsoft's security advice The first virus known to affect Microsoft Word documents was called the Concept virus, a relatively harmless virus created to demonstrate the possibility of macro virus creation.

7

Microsoft Office

Microsoft Office is a suite of productivity programs created by Microsoft and developed for Microsoft Windows and Apple Macintosh operating systems. As well as the office applications, it includes associated servers and Web-based services. Office is considered to be the *de facto* standard for productivity programs, and has many features not present in other suites. However, the reverse is also true, with other programs having capabilities Office doesn't.

Word

Microsoft Word is a word processor. It is considered to be the main program of Office. It possesses a dominant market share in the word processor market. Its proprietary DOC format is considered a de facto standard, although its most recent version, Word 11.0/2003, also supports an XML-based format. Word is also available in some editions of Microsoft Works. It is available for the Windows and Macintosh platforms. Its main competitors are OpenOffice.org Writer, StarOffice, Corel WordPerfect and Apple Pages.

Excel

Microsoft Excel is a spreadsheet program. Like Microsoft

Word, it possesses a dominant market share. It was originally a competitor to the dominant Lotus 1-2-3 but it eventually outsold it and became the de facto standard. It is available for the Windows and Macintosh platforms. Its main competitors are OpenOffice.org Calc, StarOffice and Corel Quattro Pro.

Outlook

Microsoft Outlook, not to be confused with Outlook Express, is a personal information manager and e-mail communication software. The replacement for Microsoft Mail starting in the 1997 version of Office, it includes an e-mail client, calendar, task manager and address book. Its e-mail program's main competitors are Mozilla Thunderbird/Mozilla and Eudora. Its personal information manager's main competitors are Mozilla and Lotus Organizer. It is available for Windows; a version is also included with most Pocket PC handhelds. Its Macintosh equivalent is Microsoft Entourage.

PowerPoint

Microsoft PowerPoint is a popular presentation program for Windows and Macintosh. It is used to create slideshows, composed of text, graphics, movies and other objects, which can be displayed on-screen and navigated through by the presenter or printed out on transparencies or slides. It possesses a dominant market share. Its main competitors are OpenOffice.org Impress, Corel WordPerfect and Apple Keynote. Other programs and Web-based services sometimes included

— Microsoft Access - database manager. For the 2003 version, included in Microsoft Office Professional Edition 2003, and Microsoft Office Professional Enterprise Edition 2003.

— Microsoft Binder - incorporates several documents into one file.

— Binder was a major flop for Microsoft, and is not very widely used. Newer versions of Office often do not include it for this reason.

— Microsoft Entourage - Personal information manager and communication software for Macintosh only (similar to Outlook).

— Virtual PC - emulation software; see also VMware, QEMU, Bochs, etc.

— Microsoft Publisher - Desktop publishing software. For the 2003 version, included in Microsoft Office Small Business Edition 2003, Microsoft Office Professional Edition 2003, and Microsoft Office Professional Enterprise Edition 2003.

— Microsoft FrontPage - web design software (also requires its own server program). For the 2003 version, included in Microsoft Office Professional Edition 2003, and Microsoft Office Professional Enterprise Edition 2003.

— Microsoft Internet Explorer - web browser.

— Microsoft Visio - diagram software.

— Microsoft MapPoint - mapping and travel planning software.

— Microsoft Office Picture Manager - basic photo management software (similar to a basic version of Google's Picasa or Adobe's Photoshop Elements).

— Microsoft Photo Editor - photo editing/raster graphics software in older Office versions, and again in XP. It was temporarily supplemented by Microsoft PhotoDraw in Office 2000 Premium edition.

— Microsoft Project - project manager.

— Microsoft Mail - mail client (in old versions of Office, later replaced by Microsoft Outlook).

— Microsoft Outlook Express - mail client (in Office 98 Macintosh Edition, later replaced by Microsoft Entourage).

— Microsoft OneNote - note taking software for use with tablet PCs or regular PCs.

— Microsoft InfoPath - application that enables users to design rich XML-based forms. Included in Microsoft Office Professional Enterprise Edition 2003.

— Live Communication Server - real time communication software.

— Microsoft Office Online - Web site. Included in all versions of Microsoft Office 2003.

— Microsoft Office Update - Web site. Patch detection and installation service for Office 2000, XP, and 2003.

— Microsoft Office Communicator 2005

— Developer Tools - (only included with developer editions)

Beginning with the 1997 edition, Microsoft Agent (in 9.0/2000 and up) and a similar actor technology (in 8.0/'97) have been used to provide the Office Assistant, an interactive help tool. The "Assistant" is often dubbed "Clippy" or "Clippit," due to its default to CLIPPIT.ACS. Also, beginning with Macintosh Office 1998, the Macintosh and Windows versions of Office share the same file format. Consequently, any Macintosh with Office 1998 or later can read documents created with Windows Office 8.0 or later, and vice-versa.

Office 11.0/2003 introduced a new, optional file format for the entire suite, built on XML technology. Office X for Mac is also built to handle this file format.

Microsoft develops Office primarily for Windows and secondarily for Macintosh. However, most versions of the suite can also be run on Unix-like operating systems through the use of a compatibility layer such as CrossOver Office or WINE. As a general rule of thumb, the older, simpler versions do tend to run considerably better on Wine; however, newer versions have been known to work as well.

Add ins

A major feature of applications in the Office suite is the ability for users and third party companies to write Office COM add-ins. Component Object Model (COM) add-ins are supplemental programs that extend the capabilities of an application by adding custom commands and specialized features that can accommodate specific tasks.

Trivia

For some reason, most versions of Microsoft Office (including 97 and later, and possibly 4.3) use their own widget set, and as a result do not blend in with the native operating system. Whereas Windows uses "Service Packs", Office used to release "Service Releases".

8

Microsoft Excel

Microsoft Excel is a spreadsheet program written and distributed by Microsoft for computers using the Microsoft Windows operating system and for Apple Macintosh computers. It features an intuitive interface and capable calculation and graphing tools which, along with aggressive marketing, have made Excel one of the most popular microcomputer applications to date. It is overwhelmingly the dominant spreadsheet application available for these platforms and has been so since version 5 1993 and its bundling as part of Microsoft Office.

Microsoft originally marketed a spreadsheet program called Multiplan in 1982, which was very popular on CP/M systems, but on MS-DOS systems it lost popularity to Lotus 1-2-3. This promoted development of a new spreadsheet called Excel which started with the intention to, in the words of Doug Klunder, 'do everything 1-2-3 does and do it better'. The first version of Excel was released for the Mac in 1985 and the first Windows version (numbered 2.0 to line-up with the Mac and bundled with a run-time Windows environment) was released in November 1987.

Lotus was slow to bring 1-2-3 to Windows and by 1988 Excel had started to outsell 1-2-3 and helped Microsoft achieve the position of leading PC software developer. This accomplishment, dethroning the king of the software world, solidified Microsoft as a valid competitor and showed its future of developing graphical software. Microsoft pushed its advantage with regular new releases, every two years or so. The current version is Excel 11, also called Microsoft Office Excel 2003.

Early in its life Excel became the target of a trademark lawsuit by another company already selling a software package named "Excel." As the result of the dispute Microsoft was required to refer to the program as "Microsoft Excel" in all of its formal press releases and legal documents. However, over time this practice has slipped. Excel offers a large number of user interface tweaks, however the essence of UI remains the same as in the original spreadsheet, VisiCalc: the cells are organized in rows and columns, and contain data or formulas with relative or absolute references to other cells.

Excel was the first spreadsheet that allowed the user to define the appearance of spreadsheets (fonts, character attributes and cell appearance). It also introduced intelligent cell recomputation, where only cells dependent on the cell being modified are updated, while previously spreadsheets recomputed everything all the time or waited for a specific user command. Excel has extensive graphing capabilities.

When first bundled into Microsoft Office in 1993, Microsoft Word and Microsoft PowerPoint had their GUIs redesigned for consistency with Excel, the killer app on the PC at the time. Since 1993 Excel includes support for Visual Basic for Applications (VBA) as a scripting language. VBA is a powerful tool that makes Excel a complete programming environment. VBA and macro recording allow automating routines that otherwise take several manual steps. VBA allows creating forms to handle user input. Automation functionality of VBA exposed Excel as a target for macro viruses.

Excel versions from 5.0 to 9.0 contain various Easter eggs. Versions for the Apple Macintosh include:

— 1985 Excel for Macintosh

— 1989 Excel 2.2 for Macintosh

— 1990 Excel 3.0

— 1992 Excel 4.0

— 1993 Excel 5.0

— 1998 Excel 98

— 2000 Excel 2001

— 2001 Excel v.X

— 2004 Excel 2004

Versions for MS-DOS include:

— 1987 Excel 2.0 for MS-DOS 3.0

Versions for Microsoft Windows include:

— 1987 Excel 2.0 for Windows

— 1990 Excel 3.0

— 1992 Excel 4.0

— 1993 Excel 5.0

— 1995 Excel 95 - also known as 7.0

— 1997 Excel 97 - also known as 8.0

— 1999 Excel 2000 - also known as Excel 9.0

— 2001 Excel 2002 - also known as 10.0

— 2003 Excel 2003 - also known as 11.0

9

CorelDRAW

CorelDRAW is a vector graphics editor developed and marketed by Corel Corporation of Ottawa, Canada. CorelDRAW was originally developed for Microsoft Windows but a Macintosh version was released some years later. CorelDRAW came into its own with Microsoft's release of Windows 3.1. Although a 16-bit application, the inclusion of TrueType in Windows 3.1 transformed CorelDRAW into a serious illustration program capable of quality typography. At one time, a Linux version of CorelDRAW was available, but it was subsequently discontinued. The latest version 12 is available for Windows only.

In the late 1980s, Dr. Michael Cowpland and Terry Matthews founded Corel, and hired software engineer Pat Beirne to develop an illustration program to bundle with the Intel-based desktop publishing (DTP) systems Corel was selling. The program was well received and Corel soon focused on software alone. Around the same time, as additional components were developed (Corel Trace, Corel Texture, Corel Photo-Paint, etc.) CorelDRAW was marketed as a graphics software suite.

Corel Corporation

Corel Corporation is a computer software company

headquartered in Ottawa, Ontario, Canada. It was founded by Michael Cowpland in 1985, who intended it to be a research laboratory ("Corel" is an abbreviation of "COwpland REsearch Laboratory"). The company saw great success early in the high-tech boom of the nineties with the product CorelDraw, and became, for a time, the biggest software company in Canada.

Corel made many early investors very wealthy, but its strong growth did not last. It attempted to compete with Microsoft after acquiring the WordPerfect software in 1996, but it failed badly. Corel was forced to lay-off large numbers of employees and Cowpland came under investigation by the Ontario Securities Commission for insider trading.

Concerning the WordPerfect acquisition, Cowpland believed that WordPerfect could be the "Pepsi to Microsoft's Coke". This was a classical marketing perspective, but fundamentally flawed, perhaps reflecting Cowpland's lack of expertise in the software industry. Unlike food items, software programs have strong compatibility dependencies, which make entrenched applications much harder to compete against. Even if WordPerfect were better and marketed strongly, there was simply no compelling reason for existing Microsoft Word users to switch, and new users generally want to be compatible with existing users.

Corel also failed to stop Microsoft from pushing pre-loaded copies of Word onto new computers, a strategy which eroded WordPerfect's higher market share. Because the company is no longer subject to the same rules governing publicly traded corporations, these claims can be difficult to verify. It should also be noted that many of those users received the software preloaded on a new computer. Corel generally charges the hardware manufacturer, very little per copy for bundled software.

The WordPerfect acquisition also changed the nature of Corel itself. Whereas Adobe Systems remained in the graphics and publishing software business, Corel was suddenly no longer solely within that sphere. A barrage of new projects, such as Corel Video, Barista (a Java-based office suite), Corel Computer, and Corel Linux, fueled speculation that Corel was trying to reinvent itself but wasn't sure how, or that they were "throwing stuff at the walls and looking to see what would stick." Cowpland eventually left Corel in August 2000 and a new board of directors immediately sought to stabilize operations, promising a renewed focus on the firm's core competencies.

Unfortunately, an ambitious attempt to revitalize product branding under the new president Derek Burney (with the help of consultants from McKinsey & Company) turned into a series of missteps. With great fanfare, Burney announced that the product line would be split into five brands. A few months later, it was to be three brands (DeepWhite, Procreate and Corel). And finally, after much delay and expense, it was decided that the company would go back to using "Corel" as the company's only brand.

In October 2000, Corel announced that it was forming what it called "a strategic alliance" with Microsoft and that Microsoft would be investing $135 million in Corel. In August 2003, Corel was wholly acquired by Vector Capital, a venture capital investor, for a surprisingly low price of $1 a share (about the same as the cash in the company). The company was voluntarily delisted from the NASDAQ and Toronto stock exchanges.

In March 2005 Corel announced that the US Justice Dept purchased 50,000 licences of WordPerfect (adding to the worldwide user base of 20 million) and that the WordPerfect was adding 4 million new users per year thanks to bundling deals with Dell Computer. Corel contends that WordPerfect is the only viable alternative to Microsoft Office with sales 70 times Lotus SmartSuite and 300 times Sun's Star Office.

CorelDRAW was originally developed for Microsoft Windows but a Macintosh version was released some years later. CorelDRAW came into its own with Microsoft's release of Windows 3.1. Although a 16-bit application, the inclusion of TrueType in Windows 3.1 transformed CorelDRAW into a serious illustration program capable of quality typography. At one time, a Linux version of CorelDRAW was available, but it was subsequently discontinued. The latest version 12 is available for Windows only.

In the late 1980s, Dr. Michael Cowpland and Terry Matthews founded Corel, and hired software engineer Pat Beirne to develop an illustration program to bundle with the Intel-based desktop publishing (DTP) systems Corel was selling. The program was well received and Corel soon focused on software alone. Around the same time, as additional components were developed (Corel Trace, Corel Texture, Corel Photo-Paint, etc.) CorelDRAW was marketed as a graphics software suite.

10

Adobe Illustrator

Adobe Illustrator was first developed for the Apple Macintosh in 1985 as a logical commercialization of Adobe's in-house font development software and PostScript file format. In many ways Illustrator's release was a gamble: the Macintosh did not have high market share, the only printer that could output Illustrator documents was Apple's own LaserWriter (also very new and expensive), and the drawing paradigm of Bézier curves was novel to the mainstream user. Not only did the Macintosh show only monochrome graphics, but display options were basically limited to its built-in 9" monitor. Illustrator helped drive the development of larger monitors for the Macintosh.

Illustrator was a reliable, capable product, however, and its relatively low learning curve let users quickly appreciate that the new paradigm was not only better, but finally solved the problem of imprecision from existing programs like MacDraw. It also provided a tool for people who could neither afford nor learn high-end (and perhaps overkill) software such as AutoCAD. Illustrator successfully filled a niche between painting and CAD programs. Illustrator's power and simplicity derive from the choice of Bézier curves as the primary document element.

A degenerate curve provides a line, and circles and arcs (trigonometric shapes) can be emulated closely enough. In a novel twist, Adobe also made Illustrator documents true PostScript files — if one wanted to print them, one could send them directly to a PostScript printer instead of printing them from Illustrator. Since PostScript is a readable text format, third-party developers also found it easy to write programs that generated Illustrator documents.

Illustrator 1.0 was quickly replaced by 1.1, which enjoyed widespread use. The next version (in a novel versioning scheme) was 88 (to match the year of release which was 1988). That was followed by 3.0, which provided several useful features. At around this time, Aldus had their FreeHand program available for the Macintosh, and despite having a higher learning curve, a less-polished interface, and less streamlined editing, it could do true blend fills, which kept FreeHand as a "must have" in DTP shops along with the rest of the "Big Four": Illustrator, PageMaker, and QuarkXPress.

It would be many years before Illustrator supported true blended fills, and this was perhaps the one feature that users uniformly complained was lacking. Adobe was willing to take risks with Illustrator's user interface. Instead of following Apple's UI guidelines to the letter or imitating other popular Macintosh programs, they made it possible to switch between the various navigation tools (i.e, Zoom and Pan) using various keyboard key combinations. Probably from Adobe's past experience in-house, it knew what it was doing, and the majority of users vindicated the design as "slick." Unfortunately, Apple later chose one of the key combinations (Command-Space) as the keyboard layout changer, and Windows treated another (the Alt key) as a system key.

With the introduction of Illustrator 6 in 1996, Adobe made critical changes in the user interface with regards to path editing (and also to converge on the same user interface as Adobe Photoshop), and many users opted not to upgrade. To this day, many users find the changes questionable. Illustrator also began to support TrueType, making the "font wars" between PostScript Type 1 and TrueType largely moot. Like Photoshop, Illustrator also began supporting plug-ins, greatly and quickly extending its abilities.

Although Adobe developed Illustrator primarily for the Macintosh during its first decade, it sporadically supported other platforms. In the early 1990s, Adobe released versions of Illustrator for NeXT, Silicon Graphics IRIX, and Sun Solaris platforms, but they were discontinued due to poor market acceptance. The first version of Illustrator for Microsoft Windows, version 2.0, was released in 1989, but it was a flop. The next Windows version, version 4.0, was widely criticized as being too similar to Illustrator 1.1 instead of the Macintosh 3.0 version, and certainly not the equal of Windows' most popular illustration package CorelDraw.

With true ports of the Macintosh versions to Windows starting with version 7 in 1997, designers could finally standardize on Illustrator. Corel's other problems notwithstanding (such as competing against Microsoft with WordPerfect), they relegated CorelDraw to the consumer market, as something non-professionals might use. Corel did port CorelDraw 6.0 to the Macintosh in late 1996, but it was received as too little, too late. Aldus ported FreeHand to Windows but it was not the equal of Illustrator. Adobe bought Aldus in 1994 for PageMaker, and as part of the transaction it sold FreeHand to Macromedia.

With the rise of the Internet, Illustrator was enhanced to support Web publishing, rasterization previewing, PDF, and SVG, all welcome additions. For reasons unknown, Adobe has chosen to license Sandro Botticelli's "The Birth of Venus" from the Bettmann Archive and use the portion containing Venus' face as Illustrator's branding image. Over the years, the rendition of this image on Illustrator's splash screen has become more refined as Illustrator gains new features. It's reasonable to assume that Adobe wanted Illustrator to be perceived as a professional product for discriminating artists.

Adobe Illustrator is currently at version 12 (called CS2 to reflect its integration with Adobe's Creative Suite) and is available for both the Mac OS X and Microsoft Windows operating systems. The image of Venus was replaced in Illustrator CS (version 11) with a stylized flower(s).

11

Desktop Publishing

Desktop publishing, or DTP, is the process of editing and layout of printed material intended for publication, such as books, magazines, brochures, and the like using a personal computer. Desktop publishing software, such as QuarkXPress or Adobe InDesign, is software specifically designed for such tasks. Such programs do not generally replace word processors and graphics applications, but are used to aggregate content created in these programs: text, raster graphics (such as images edited with Adobe Photoshop) and vector graphics (such as drawings/ illustrations made with Adobe Illustrator). When the material is ready for publication the DTP software can output PostScript or Adobe PDF which can be used by the commercial printers to produce printing plates.

Desktop publishing started in 1985, with the conjunction of Aldus Pagemaker (later acquired by Adobe), the Apple Macintosh, and the $7000 Apple LaserWriter, the first laser printer to use Adobe Systems' PostScript page description language, including its scalable fonts in Type 1 format. The phrase desktop publishing is attributed to Paul Brainerd, the founder of Aldus Corporation, as a marketing term that referred to the use of a computer on top of a desk for publishing and also alluded the desktop metaphor that Apple used to mimic a real desktop.

In 1986 Ventura Publisher was introduced on the PC moving infant DTP into the mainstream, this allowed DTP to be moved into the home market via GST's Timeworks Publisher on the PC and Atari ST but these systems were initially used mainly for small-distribution publications such as club newsletters. While this allowed many more people access to publishing their own work it also gave DTP a bad reputation for a while as amateurs made typographical mistakes that professional typesetters would never make.

As these systems improved they became widely adopted throughout the professional publishing world. The turning point was the introduction of Quark XPress 3.0 in the 1990s-currently, virtually all publishing is "desktop publishing." The superior flexibility and speed of desktop publishing systems has greatly reduced the lead time for magazine publication and allowed more elaborate layouts than would otherwise have been possible. Programmable, automated systems like LaTeX mean that long, repetitive, or highly-structured documents can be produced in a fraction of the time that it would take a manually-controlled system.

Computer based typesetting using a personal computer started in 1978, when the TeX program showed that publication-quality typesetting could be done on any normal business computer, and even long and complex jobs like books and journals could be produced from a standard desktop terminal. Prior to this, typesetting had been performed by mechanical (Lintotype and Monotype) or electro-mechanical means (photofilmsetting), or by extremely expensive mainframe or mini-computer based systems. The introduction of the Apple Macintosh and PageMaker allowed synchronous typographical editing using the graphical user interface, this system was commonly referred to as What You See is What You Get, WYSIWYG.

The Apple Macintosh, with historically superior graphics capabilities (particularly in the areas of typography and colour management), and a simple GUI, is highly popular in this application domain and remains one of Apple's core markets. The Atari TT030 was widely used for DTP with Calamus application. Calamus has its own technology called Softripping for WYSIWYG which uses the same routine for output to monitor as well as high density print devices.

Adobe PageMaker

PageMaker was the first desktop publishing program, introduced in 1985 by Aldus Corporation, initially for the Apple Macintosh but soon after also for the PC. It relies on Adobe Systems' PostScript page description language. In 1994 Aldus Corporation and PageMaker were acquired by Adobe Systems. The current version is PageMaker 7.0, released July 9, 2001, though updates have been released for the two supported platforms since.

Many of the graphical user interface (GUI) elements pioneered in the program have since migrated to the rest of the Adobe suite. Adobe has positioned PageMaker to compete more for the small business market, with Adobe InDesign aimed at the high end, professional designer. PageMaker's feature set is well suited for publications such as corporate newsletters and the straight-news sections of newspapers, but for layouts that need a more complex design, such as magazines or the feature sections of newspapers, it may take much longer to accomplish the task in PageMaker than it would in InDesign or QuarkXPress, if the desired results are possible at all.

While PageMaker is less powerful than InDesign or QuarkXPress, it is simpler to learn than those two packages and yet more powerful than Microsoft Publisher.

12

Computer Graphics

Computer graphics (CG) is the field of visual computing, where one utilizes computers both to generate visual images synthetically and to integrate or alter visual and spatial information sampled from the real world. The first major advance in computer graphics was the development of the Sketchpad in 1962 by Ivan Sutherland.

This field can be divided into several areas: real-time 3D rendering (often used in video games), computer animation, video capture and video creation rendering, special effects editing (often used for movies and television), image editing, and modeling (often used for engineering and medical purposes). Development in computer graphics was first fueled by academic interests and government sponsorship. However, as real-world applications of computer graphics (CG) in broadcast television and movies proved a viable alternative to more traditional special effects and animation techniques, commercial parties have increasingly funded advances in the field.

It is often thought that the first feature film to use computer graphics was 2001: A Space Odyssey, which attempted to show how computers would be much more graphical in the future. However, all the "computer graphic" effects in that film were hand-drawn animation, and the special effects sequences were produced entirely with conventional optical and model effects. Perhaps the first use of computer graphics specifically to illustrate computer graphics was in Futureworld, which included an animation of a human face and hand - produced by Ed Catmull and Fred Parke at the University of Utah.

2D Computer Graphics

The first advance in computer graphics was in the use of CRTs. See 2D computer graphics. There are two approaches to 2D graphics: vector and raster graphics. Vector graphics stores precise geometric data, topology and style such as coordinate positions of points, the connections between points (to form lines or paths) and the colour, thickness and possible fill of the shapes. Most vector graphic systems can also use primitives of standard shapes such as circles and rectangles etc. In most cases a vector graphic image has to be converted to a raster image to be viewed.

Raster graphics is a uniform two dimensional grid of pixels. Each pixel has a specific value such as for instance brightness, colour transparancy or a combination of such values. A raster image has a finite resolution of a specific number of rows and columns. Standard computer displays shows a raster image of resolutions such as 1280(columns)x1024(rows) of pixels. Today one often combines raster and vector graphics in compound file formats (pdf,swf).

3D Computer Graphics

With the birth of the workstation computers (like LISP machines, paintbox computers and Silicon Graphics workstations) came the 3D computer graphics, based on vector graphics. Instead of the computer storing information about points, lines and curves on a 2-

Dimensional plane, the computer stores the location of points, lines and typically faces (to construct a polygon) in 3-Dimensional Space.

3-Dimensional polygons are the life blood of virtally all 3D computer graphics. As a result, most 3D graphics engines are based around storing points (single 3 Dimensional coordinates,) lines that connect those points togather, and faces between the lines, and then a sequence of faces to create 3D polygons.Modern day computer graphics software goes far beyond just the simple storage of polygons in computer memory. Today's graphics are not only the product of massive collections of polygons into recognizable shapes, they also result from techniques in shading, texturing and rasterization

Shading

The process of shading (in the context of 3D computer graphics) involves the computer simulating (or more accurately; calculating) how the faces of a polygon will look when illuminated by a virtual light source. The exact calculation varies depending on not only what data is availble about the face being shaded, but also the shading technique.

— *Flat shading*: A technique that shades each polygon of an object based on the polygon's "normal" and the position and intensity of a light source.

— *Gouraud shading*: Invented by Henri Gouraud in 1971, a fast and resource-conscious technique used to simulate smoothly shaded surfaces by interpolating vertex colors across a polygon's surface.

— *Texture mapping*: A technique for simulating surface detail by mapping images (textures) onto polygons.

— *Phong shading*: Invented by Bui Tuong Phong, a smooth shading technique that approximates curved-surface lighting by interpolating the vertex normals of a polygon across the surface; the lighting model includes glossy reflection with a controlable level of gloss.

— *Bump mapping*: Invented by Jim Blinn, a normal-perturbation technique used to simulate bumpy or wrinkled surfaces.

— Ray Tracing: A method based on the physical principles of geometric optics that can simulate multiple reflections and transparency.

— *Radiosity*: a technique for global illumination that uses radiative transfer theory to simulate indirect (reflected) illumination in scenes with diffuse surfaces.

— *Blobs*: a technique for representing surfaces without specifing a hard boundary representation, usually implemented as a procedural surface like a Van-der-Vaals equipotential (in chemistry).

Texturing

Polygon surfaces (the sequence of faces) can contain data corresponding to not only a color, but in more advanced software, can be a virtual canvas for a picture, or other rasterized image. Such an image is placed onto a face, or series of faces and is called a Texture. Textures add a new degree of customization as to how a faces & polygons will ultimately look after being shaded, depending on the shading method, and how the image is interpreted during shading.

Raster Graphics

Suppose the smiley face in the top left corner is an RGB bitmap image. When zoomed in, it might look like the big smiley face to the right. Every square represents a pixel. Zoomed in further we see three pixels whose colors are constructed by adding the values for red, green and blue. A raster graphics image, digital image, or bitmap, is a data file or structure representing a generally rectangular grid of pixels, or points of color, on a computer monitor, paper, or other display device. The color of each pixel is individually defined; images in the RGB color space, for instance, often consist of colored pixels defined by three bytes-one byte each for red, green and blue.

Less colorful images require less information per pixel; an image with only black and white pixels requires only a single bit for each pixel. Raster graphics are distinguished from vector graphics in that vector graphics represent an image through the use of geometric objects such as curves and polygons. A bitmap corresponds bit for bit with an image displayed on a screen, probably in the same format as it would be stored in the display's video memory or maybe as a device independent bitmap. A bitmap is characterized by the width and height of the image in pixels and the number of bits per pixel, which determines the number of colors it can represent.

A colored raster image (or pixmap) will usually have pixels with between one and eight bits for each of the red, green, and blue components, though other color encodings are also used, such as four- or eight-bit indexed representations that use vector quantization on the (R, G, B) vectors. The green component sometimes has more bits than the other two to allow for the human eye's greater discrimination in this component.

The quality of a raster image is determined by the total number of pixels (resolution), and the amount of information in each pixel (often called color depth). For example, an image that stores 24 bits of color information per pixel (the standard for all displays since around 1995) can represent smoother degrees of shading than one that only stores 16 bits per pixel, but not as smooth as one that stores 48 bits (technically; this would not be decipherable by the human eye). Likewise, an image sampled at 640 x 480 pixels (therefore containing 307,200 pixels) will look rough and blocky compared to one sampled at 1280 x 1024 (1,310,720 pixels). Because it takes a large amount of data to store a high-quality image, data compression techniques are often used to reduce this size for images stored on disk.

Some techniques sacrifice information, and therefore image quality, in order to achieve a smaller file size. Compression techniques that lose information are referred to as "lossy" compression. Raster graphics cannot be scaled to a higher resolution without loss of apparent quality. This is in contrast to vector graphics, which easily scale to the quality of the device on which they are rendered. Raster graphics are more practical than vector graphics for photographs and photo-realistic images, while vector graphics are often more practical for typesetting or graphic design.

Early 21st century computer monitors typically display about 72 to 130 pixels per inch (PPI), and some modern consumer printers can resolve 2400 dots per inch (DPI) or more; determining the most appropriate image resolution for a given printer resolution can be difficult, since printed output may have a greater level of detail than can be discerned on a monitor.

In 3D computer graphics, the concept of a flat raster of pixels is sometimes extended to a three dimensional volume of voxels. In this case, there is a regular grid in three dimensional space with a sample containing color information at each point in the grid. Although voxels are powerful abstractions for dealing with complex 3D shapes, they do have large memory requirements for storing a sizable array. Consequently, vector graphics are used more frequently than voxels for producing 3D imagery.

Raster graphics was first patented by Texas Instruments in the 1970s, and is now ubiquitous. Vector graphics or geometric modeling is the use of geometrical primitives such as points, lines, curves, and polygons to represent images in computer graphics. It is used by contrast to the term raster graphics, which is the representation of images as a collection of pixels.

13

Use of Colours in Printing

A colour model is an abstract mathematical model describing the way colours can be represented as tuples of numbers, typically as three or four values or colour components (e.g. RGB and CMYK are colour models). However, a colour model with no associated mapping function to a reference colour space is a more or less arbitrary colour system with little connection to the requirements of any given application.

Adding a certain mapping function between the colour model and a certain reference colour space results in a definite "footprint" within the reference colour space. This "footprint" is known as a gamut, and, in combination with the colour model, defines a new colour space. For example, Adobe RGB and sRGB are two different colour spaces, both based on the RGB model.

All colours can be created by the primary colours red, blue, and yellow, if working with paints. Those colours are then a colour space. We can see the amount of red colour as the X axis, the amount of blue as the Y axis, and the amount of yellow as the Z axis. We now have a 3D space, wherein every possible colour has a given position.

However, this is not the only colour space around. For instance, when colours are displayed on a computer monitor, they are usually called RGB, for red, green and blue. This is another way of making the same colours, and red, green and blue can be considered as the X, Y and Z axis. Another way of making the same colours is to use their hue (X axis), their saturation (Y axis) and their brightness (z axes). This is called the HSB colour space. And there are many more colour spaces. Many can be represented as 3D (X,Y,Z) values in this way, but some have more, or less dimensions, and some cannot be represented in this way at all.

"Colour space" is a more specific term for a certain combination of a colour model plus a colour mapping function, the term "colour space" tends to be used to also identify colour models, since identifying a colour space automatically identifies the associated colour model. Informally, the two terms are often used interchangeably, though this is strictly incorrect. For example, although several specific colour spaces are based on the RGB model, there is no such thing as the RGB colour space.

The RGB colour model is implemented in different ways, depending on the capabilities of the system used. By far the most common general-use incarnation as of 2005 is the 24-bit implementation, with 8 bits, or 256 discrete levels of colour per channel. Any colour space based on such a 24-bit RGB model is thus limited to a gamut of 256×256×256 ˜ 16.7 million colours. Some implementations use 16 bits per component, resulting in the same range with a greater density of distinct colours. This is especially important when working with wide-gamut colour spaces (where most of the more common colours are located relatively close together), or when a large number of digital filtering algorithms are used consecutively. The same principle applies for any colour spaces based on the same colour model, but implemented in different bit depths.

Purpose Colour Spaces

The RG Chromaticity space is used in Computer vision applications, and shows the colour of light (red, yellow, green etc.), but not its intensity (dark, bright). Early colour spaces had two components. They largely ignored blue light because the added complexity of a 3-component process provided much less of a marginal increase in fidelity than the jump from monochrome to 2-component colour.

— RG for early Technicolour film

— RGK for early colour printing

Additive Colour

An additive colour system involves light emitted directly from a source or illuminant of some sort. The additive reproduction process usually uses red, green and blue light to produce the other colours. Combining one of these additive primary colours with another in equal amounts produces the additive secondary colours cyan, magenta, and yellow. Combining all three primary colours in equal intensities produces white. Varying the luminosity of each light eventually reveals the full gamut of those 3 lights. Computer monitors and televisions are the most common application of additive colour. James Clerk Maxwell is credited as being the father of additive colour.

Subtractive Colour

Subtractive colour explains the theory of mixing paints, dyes, inks, and natural colourants to create colours which absorb some wavelengths of light and reflect others. The colour that an object appears to have is based on what parts of the spectrum are reflected by it, or conversely by what parts of the spectrum are not absorbed. Anything that is not additive colour is subtractive colour. No other colour mixing systems are known, except the imperfect system resulting from mixing real pigments, something that is very confusing nowadays. Colour is not an absolute, but depends on the details of human colour vision, which varies between individuals. Although colour can be measured by instruments, such instruments are simply emulating a particular individual's vision.

Colour Mixing

RGB uses additive colour mixing, because it describes what kind of light needs to be emitted to produce a given colour. Light is added together to create form from out of the darkness. RGB stores individual values for red, green and blue. RGBA is RGB with an additional channel, alpha, to indicate transparency. Colour spaces based on the RGB model include sRGB, Adobe RGB and Adobe Wide Gamut RGB.

CMYK uses subtractive colour mixing used in the printing process, because it describes what kind of inks need to be applied so the light reflected from them produces a given colour. One starts with a white canvas, and uses ink to subtract colour from white to create an image. CMYK stores ink values for cyan, magenta, yellow and black.

YIQ is used in NTSC (North American) television broadcasts for historical reasons. YIQ stores a luminance value with two chrominance values, corresponding approximately to the amounts of blue and red in the colour. It corresponds closely to the YUV scheme used in PAL television except that the YIQ colour space is rotated 33° with respect to the YUV colour space. The YDbDr scheme used by SECAM television is rotated in another way. YPbPr is a scaled version of YUV. It is most commonly seen in its digital form, YCbCr, used widely in video and image compression schemes such as MPEG and JPEG.

HSV is often used by artists because it is often more natural to think about a colour in terms of hue and saturation than in terms of additive or subtractive colour components. HSV stores a hue value, a saturation value and an intensity value. HLS is quite similar to HSV, with lightness replacing intensity value.

The main reason that black ink (as in CMYK) is used in addition to cyan, magenta, and yellow, is that the latter inks usually cannot be combined to create a true black. No coloured inks will absorb all wavelengths which might appear reddish, for example, meaning that all practical CMY mixtures, mixed at full intensity, will produce an off-black result. The coloured inks are therefore printed first to produce the hue, while the black ink is used to produce the value.

Primary Colour

A primary colour (or colour) is a colour that cannot be created by mixing other colours in the gamut of a given colour space. Primary colours may themselves be mixed to produce most of the colours in a given colour space. Traditionally, the colours red, yellow, and blue are considered to be primary pigments. This is simply incorrect, however. If the colour space is considered as a vector space, the primary colours can be regarded as a set of basis vectors for that space.

Primary colours are not a physical but rather a biological concept, based on the physiological response of the human eye to light. The human eye contains receptors called cones which normally respond to red, green, and blue light. Humans and other species with three such types of colour receptors are known as trichromats. Although the peak responsivities of the cones do not occur exactly at the red, green and blue frequencies, those three colours are chosen as primary because they provide a wide gamut, making it possible to almost independently stimulate the three colour receptors.

To generate optimal colour ranges for species other than humans, other additive primary colours would have to be used. For species known as tetrachromats with four different colour receptors, one would use four primary colours. Many birds and marsupials are tetrachromats and it has been suggested that some female humans are born as tetrachromats as well, having an extra receptor for yellow. On the other hand, most mammals have only two types of colour receptors and are therefore dichromats; to them, there are only two primary colours.

Media that use reflected light and colourants to produce colours are using the subtractive colour method of colour mixing. In the printing industry, to produce the varying colours, apply the subtractive primaries yellow, cyan, and magenta together in varying amounts. Subtractive colour works best when the surface (or paper) is white, or close to it.

Mixing yellow and cyan produces shades of green; mixing yellow with magenta produces shades of red, and mixing magenta with cyan produces shades of blue. In theory, mixing equal amounts of all three pigments should produce shades of grey, resulting in black when all three are fully saturated, but in practice they tend to produce muddy brown colours. For this reason, a fourth "primary" pigment, black, is often used in addition to the cyan, magenta, and yellow colours. The colour space generated is the so-called CMYK colour space (standing for "Cyan, Magenta, Yellow, and Black - K is used to represent black as 'B' could be confused with 'Blue'").

In practice, mixtures of actual materials like paint tend to be less precise. Brighter, or more specific colours can be created using natural pigments instead of mixing, and natural properties of pigments can interfere with the mixing. For example, mixing magenta and green in acrylic creates a dark cyan - something which would not happen if the mixing process were perfectly subtractive. In the subtractive model, adding white to a colour does not change its hue but does reduce its saturation.

CMYK Colour Model

CMYK (or sometimes YMCK) is a subtractive colour model used in colour printing. This colour model is based on mixing pigments of the following colours in order to make other colours:

— C=Cyan

— M=Magenta

— Y=Yellow

— K=Key (black).

The mixture of ideal CMY colours is subtractive (Cyan, Magenta, and Yellow printed together on white result to black). CMYK works through light absorption. The colours that are seen are from the part of light that is not absorbed. In CMYK magenta plus yellow produces red, magenta plus cyan makes blue, cyan plus yellow generates green and the combination of cyan, magenta, and yellow form black. For several reasons, the 'black' generated by mixing the subtractive primaries is not ideal and so four-colour printing uses black ink in addition to the subtractive primaries yellow, magenta, and cyan. The reasons for using black ink include

— A mixture of cyan, magenta, and yellow is not pure black, but a dark murky colour.

— Mixing all three process colour inks together merely to make black can make the paper rather wet, which is an issue in high speed printing where the paper must dry extremely rapidly to avoid marking the next sheet, and poor quality paper such as newsprint may break if it becomes too wet

— Text is typically printed in black and includes fine detail (such as serifs); so to reproduce text using three inks without slight blurring would require impractically accurate registration (i.e. all three images would need to be positioned extremely precisely)

— Using a unit amount of black ink rather than three unit amounts of the process colour inks can lead to significant cost savings, especially because black ink can be less expensive than any of the colour inks.

The amount of black to use to replace amounts of the other ink is variable, and the choice depends on the technology, paper and ink in use. Processes called under colour removal, under colour addition, and grey component replacement are used to decide on the final mix, so that different CMYK recipes will be used depending on the printing task. Where black is mixed with the other colours, this is "blacker than black" and is referred to as rich black.

Use of four-colour printing generates a good final printed result with greater contrast. However the colour a person sees on a computer screen is often somewhat different from the colour of the same object on a printout since CMYK and the RGB colour model used in computer monitors have different gamuts. For example, dark blue reproduces poorly in CMYK, coming out rather murky (as it has to be approximated by darkening cyan with black and a little magenta).

Colour Printing

Printing is an industrial process for reproducing copies of texts and images, typically with ink on paper using a printing press. It is an essential part of publishing. Books are usually printed today using the technique of offset printing, and occasionally relief print, (which is principally used for newspapers and catalogues). The largest commercial and industrial printer in the world is Montréal, Quebec based Quebecor World.

History of Printing

Printing was first discovered and developed in China. Primitive Woodblock printing was already in use by the 6th century BC. The oldest surviving book printed using the more sophisticated block printing dates from 868 AD (The Diamond Sutra of AD 868, a Buddhist scripture). The movable type printer was invented by Pi Sheng in 1040. The movable type metal printing press was invented in Korea between 1234 and 1241. By the 12th and 13th century many Arabic and Chinese libraries contained tens of thousands of printed books.

There is little direct evidence, but it is highly probable that Chinese printing technology diffused into Europe through trade links that went through India and on through the Arabic world. Johann Gutenberg, of the German city of Mainz, developed European printing technology in 1440. Basing the design of his machine on a wine press, Gutenberg developed the use of raised and movable type and from the start used oil based inks.

This development of the printing press revolutionized the spread of knowledge: a printing press was built in Venice in 1469, and the city had 417 printers by 1500. In 1476, a printing press was developed in England by William Caxton; in 1539, the Italian Juan Pablos set up an imported press in Mexico City, Mexico. Stephen Day built the first printing press in North America at Massachusetts Bay in 1628, and helped establish the Cambridge Press.

In Prints and Visual Communication, William Ivins offers the following concise history of a series of rapid innovations in image and type printing at the end of the eighteenth century: At the end of the eighteenth century there were several remarkable innovations in the graphic techniques and those that were utilized to make their materials. Bewick developed the method of using engraving tools on the end of the wood. Senefelder discovered lithography. Blake made relief etchings. Early in the nineteenth century Stanhope, George E. Clymer, Koenig and others introduced new kinds of type presses, which for strength surpassed anything that had previously been known.

Computer Printing

A document can also be printed by a laser printer, inkjet, or other computer printer. In recent years, computer printing and industrial printing processes have converged, leading to the development of digital printing and on-demand printing. The artistic process of printmaking is also known as printing, as is photographic printing.

Colour printing involves a series of steps, or transformations, in order to generate a quality colour reproduction. Here are the main steps when reproducing a colour image in CMYK print, along with some historical perspective.

Colour Separation Process

The process of colour separation occurs when the original artwork is digitally scanned and separated into red, green, and blue components. Before digital imaging was developed, the traditional method of doing this was to photograph the image three times, using a filter for each colour. However this is achieved, the desired result is three grayscale images, which represent the red, green, and blue (RGB) components of the original image:

The next step is to invert each of these separations. When a negative image of the red component is produced, the resulting image represents the cyan component of the image. Likewise, negatives are produced of the green and blue components to produce magenta and yellow separations, respectively. This is done because cyan, magenta, and yellow are subtractive primaries which each represent two of the three additive primaries (RGB) after one additive primary has been subtracted from white light.

Today's digital printing methods do not have the restriction of a single colour space that traditional CMYK processes do. Many presses can print from files that were ripped with images using either RGB or CMYK modes. The colour reproduction abilities of a particular colour space can vary; the process of obtaining accurate colours within a colour model is called colour matching.

Screening

Printing inks cannot mix, or commingle. For this reason, only one colour of ink can be allowed to be on a particular point of the paper at a time. The optical illusion created by the colours being so close together gives the viewer the impression of a continuous-tone image. Keeping the colours separate from each other is accomplished by using a screen, also known as a halftone.

Final Composite Image

Traditionally, halftone screens were generated by inked lines on two sheets of glass that were cemented together at right angles. Each of the colour separation films were then exposed through these screens. The resulting high-contrast image, once processed, had dots of varying diameter depending on the amount of exposure that area received, which was modulated by the grayscale separation film image.

The glass screens were obsoleted by high-contrast films where the halftone dots were exposed with the separation film. This in turn was replaced by a process where the halftones are electronically generated directly on the film with a laser. Most recently, Computer To Plate (CTP) technology has allowed printers to bypass the film portion of the process entirely. CTP images the dots directly on the printing plate with a laser, saving money, increasing quality (by reducing the repeated generations), reducing lead-times, and saving the environment from toxic film processing chemicals.

Screens with a ruling of 60 to 120 lines per inch (lpi) are used to reproduce colour photographs in newspapers. This does not give high-quality reproduction, but this is the best halftoning possible on the cheap, highly absorbent paper used. A finer screen would lead to the ink spreading and the colours being muddied. A good way to see halftoning in action is to examine a colour newspaper image with a magnifying glass. Screens with 133 to 175 lpi are used for magazines and commercial printing.

Stochastic Screening

Digital imaging technology has also given rise to new approaches to the screening process. The best-known is stochastic screening. Because the dots are the same size and randomly placed, the moiré effects that are generated by traditional half-tones are eliminated. A side benefit of stochastic screening is the ability obtain a wider gamut of colours using additional inks such as orange or green (hexachrome).

Due to the high resolution of the screen, using Computer-To-Plate imaging gives optimal results. Almost all inkjet devices use stochastic screening. Take a magnifier (or loupe) if you own an inkjet printer at home and take a peek at any image you've printed. Stochastic screening or some hybrid of traditional linescreen and stochastic has become the standard screening method for many packaging application.

Digital Image Processing

Digital image processing is the use of algorithms to perform image processing on digital images. Digital image processing has the same advantages as digital signal processing in that it allows a much wider range of algorithms to be applied to the input data, and can avoid problems such as the build-up of noise and signal distortion during processing. Because of the computational load of dealing with images containing millions of pixels, digital image processing was largely of academic interest until the 1970s, when dedicated hardware became available that could process images in real time, for some dedicated problems such as television standards conversion.

As general-purpose computers became faster, they started to take over the role of dedicated hardware for all but the most specialized and compute-intensive operations. With the fast computers and signal processors available in the 2000s, digital image processing has become the commonest form of image processing, and is generally used because it is not only the most versatile method, but also the cheapest.

Digital image processing allows the use of much more complex algorithms for image processing, and hence can offer both more sophisticated performance at simple tasks, and the implementation of methods which would be impossible by analog means. In particular, digital image processing is the only practical technology for:

— Classification

— Feature extraction

— Pattern recognition

— Projection

— Multi-scale signal analysis

Some techniques which are used in digital image processing include:

— Principal components analysis

— Independent component analysis

— Self-organizing maps

— Hidden Markov models

— Neural networks

14

Networks, Communications and the Internet

After ARPANET had been up and running for a decade, ARPA looked for another agency to hand off the network to. After all, ARPA's primary business was funding cutting-edge research and development, not running a communications utility. Eventually the network was turned over to the Defense Communications Agency, also part of the Department of Defense. In 1983, TCP/IP protocols replaced the earlier NCP protocol as the principal protocol of the ARPANET; in 1984, the U.S. military portion of the ARPANet was broken off as a separate network, the MILNET.

The early Internet, based around the ARPANET, was government-funded and therefore restricted to non-commercial uses such as research; unrelated commercial use was strictly forbidden. This initially restricted connections to military sites and universities. During the 1980s, the connections expanded to more educational institutions, and even to a growing number of companies such as Digital Equipment Corporation and Hewlett-Packard, which were participating in research projects, or providing services to those who were.

Another branch of the U.S. government, the National Science Foundation, became heavily involved in Internet research in the mid-1980s. The NSFNet backbone, intended to connect and provide access to a number of supercomputing centers established by the NSF, was established in 1986. At the end of the 1980s, the U.S. Department of Defense decided the network was developed enough for its initial purposes, and decided to stop further funding of the core Internet backbone. The ARPANET was gradually shut down (its last node was turned off in 1989), and NSF, a civilian agency, took over responsibility for providing long-haul connectivity in the U.S.

In another NSF initiative, regional TCP/IP-based networks such as NYSERNet (New York State Education and Research Network) and BARRNet (Bay Area Regional Research Network), grew up and started interconnecting with the nascent Internet. This greatly expanded the reach of the rapidly growing network. On April 30, 1995 the NSF privatized access to the network they had created. It was at this point that the growth of the Internet really took off.

Commercialization and Privatization

Parallel to the Internet, other networks were growing. Some were educational and centrally-organized like BITNET and CSNET. Others were a grass-roots mix of school, commercial, and hobby like the UUCP network. During the late 1980s the first Internet Service Provider (ISP) companies were formed. Companies like PSINet, UUNET, Netcom, and Portal were formed to provide service to the regional research networks and provide alternate network access (like UUCP-based email and Usenet News) to the public.

The interest in commercial use of the Internet became a hotly-debated topic. Although commercial use was forbidden, the exact definition of commercial use could be unclear and subjective. Everyone agreed that one company sending an invoice to another company was clearly commercial use, but anything less was up for debate. The alternate networks, like UUCP, had no such restrictions, so many people were skirting grey areas in the interconnection of the various networks.

Many university users were outraged at the idea of non-educational use of their networks. Ironically it was the commercial Internet service providers who brought prices low enough that junior colleges and other schools could afford to participate in the new arenas of education and research. By 1994, the NSFNet lost its standing as the backbone of the Internet. Other competing commercial providers created their own backbones and interconnections. Regional NAPs (network access points) became the primary interconnections between the many networks. The NSFNet was dropped as the main backbone, and commercial restrictions were gone.

Early Applications

E-mail existed as a message service on early time-sharing mainframe computers connected to a number of terminals. Around 1971 it developed into the first system of exchanging addressed messages between different, networked computers; in 1972 Ray Tomlinson introduced the "name@computer" notation that is still used today. E-mail turned into the Internet "killer application" of the 1980s. The early e-mail system was not limited to the Internet. Gateway machines connected Internet SMTP e-mail with UUCP mail, BITNET, the Fidonet BBS network, and other services. Commercial e-mail providers such as CompuServe and The Source could also be reached.

The second most popular application of the early Internet was Usenet, a system of distributed discussion groups which is still going strong today. Usenet had existed even before the internet, as an application of Unix computers connected by telephone lines via UUCP. The Network News Transfer Protocol (NNTP), similar in flavor to SMTP, slowly replaced UUCP for the relaying of news articles. Today, almost all Usenet traffic is carried over high-speed NNTP servers. Other early protocols include the File Transfer Protocol, and Telnet, a networked terminal emulator allowing users on one computer to log in to other computers.

One of the scalability limitations of the early Internet was that there was no distributed way to name hosts, other than with their IP addresses. The Network Information Centre (NIC) maintained a central hosts file, giving names for various reachable hosts. Sites were expected to download this file regularly to have a current list of hosts. In 1984, Paul Mockapetris devised the Domain Name System (DNS) as an alternative. Domain names provided names for hosts that were both globally unique (like IP addresses), memorable (like hostnames), and distributed — sites no longer had to download a hosts file. Domain names quickly became a feature of e-mail addresses — replacing the older bang path notation — as well as other services.

The Internet has developed a significant subculture dedicated to the idea that the Internet is not owned or controlled by any one person, company, group, or organization. Nevertheless, some standardization and control is necessary for anything to function. Many people wanted to put their ideas into the standards for communication between the computers that made up this network, so a system was devised for putting forward ideas. One would write one's ideas in a paper called a "Request for Comments" (RFC for short), and let everyone else read it. People commented on and improved those ideas in new RFCs.

With its basis as an educational research project, much of the documentation was written by students or others who played significant roles in developing the network (as part of the original Network Working Group) but did not have official responsibility for defining standards. This is the reason for the very low-key name of "Request for Comments" rather than something like "Declaration of Official Standards". The first RFC (RFC1) was written on April 7th, 1969. As of 2004 there are over 3500 RFCs, describing every aspect of how the Internet functions.

The liberal RFC publication procedure has engendered confusion about the Internet standardization process, and has led to more formalization of official accepted standards. Acceptance of an RFC by the RFC Editor for publication does not automatically make the RFC into a standard. It may be recognized as such by the IETF only after many years of experimentation, use, and acceptance have proven it to be worthy of that designation. Official standards are numbered with a prefix "STD" and a number, similar to the RFC naming style. However, even after becoming a standard, most are still commonly referred to by their RFC number.

The Internet standards process has been as innovative as the Internet technology. Prior to the Internet, standardization was a slow process run by committees with arguing vendor-driven factions and lengthy delays. In networking in particular, the results were monstrous patchworks of bloated specifications. The fundamental requirement for a networking protocol to become an Internet standard is the existence of at least two existing, working implementations that inter-operate with each other. This makes sense in retrospect, but it was a new concept at the time.

Other efforts built huge specifications with many optional parts and then expected people to go off and implement them, and only later did people find that they did not inter-operate, or worse, the standard was completely impossible to implement. In the 1980s, the International Organization for Standardization (ISO) documented a new effort in networking called Open Systems Interconnect or OSI. Prior to OSI, networking was completely vendor-developed and proprietary. OSI was a new industry effort, attempting to get everyone to agree to common network standards to provide multi-vendor interoperability. The OSI model was the most important advance in teaching network concepts.

However, the OSI protocols or "stack" that were specified as part of the project were a bloated mess. Standards like X.400 for e-mail took up several large books, while Internet e-mail took only a few dozen pages at most in RFC-821 and 822. Most protocols and specifications in the OSI stack, such as token-bus media, CLNP packet delivery, FTAM file transfer, and X.400 e-mail, are long-gone today; in 1996, ISO finally acknowledged that TCP/IP had won and killed the OSI project. Only one OSI standard, X.500 directory service, still survives with significant usage, mainly because the original unwieldy protocol has been stripped away and effectively replaced with LDAP. Some formal organization is necessary to make everything operate. The first central authority was the NIC (Network Information Centre) at SRI (Stanford Research Institute in Menlo Park, California).

World Wide Web

One of the Internet applications many people are most familiar with is the World Wide Web. As the Internet grew through the 1980s and early 1990s, many people realized the growing need to be able to find and organize files and related information. Projects such as Gopher, WAIS, and the Anonymous FTP Archive Site list attempted to create schemes to organize distributed data and present it to people in an easy-to-use form. Unfortunately, these projects fell short in being able to accommodate all the various existing file and data types, and in being able to grow without centralized bottlenecks. Gopher's development would later be halted when the University of Minnesota asserted its intellectual property rights over the technology.

Meanwhile, one of the most promising user interface paradigms during this period was hypertext. The technology's creation had been inspired by Vannevar Bush's "memex" and developed through Ted Nelson's research on Project Xanadu and Douglas Engelbart's research on NLS_(computer_system). Many small self-contained hypertext systems had been created before, such as Apple Computer's HyperCard, but before the Internet, nobody had worked out how to scale up the technology so that it could to refer to another document anywhere in the world. Both Nelson and one of Engelbart's collaborators had speculated about how to do it, but such speculations had gone nowhere.

The actual solution was invented by Tim Berners-Lee in 1989, out of sheer exasperation after he kept raising his idea at conferences and no one in the Internet or hypertext communities would implement it for him. He was a computer programmer working at CERN, the European Particle Physics Laboratory, and wanted a way for physicists to share information about their research. His documentation project was the source of the two key inventions that made the World Wide Web possible. These two inventions were the Uniform Resource Locator (URL) and HyperText Markup Language (HTML).

The URL was a simple way to specify the location of a document anywhere on the Internet in one simple name that specified a computer name, a file "path" on that machine, and a protocol to use in retrieving that file. HTML was an easy way to embed codes into a text file that could define the structure of a document and also include links pointing to other documents. An additional network protocol, (HTTP), was also invented for reduced overhead and improved speed during file transfers, but the true genius of the new system was that a new protocol was useful but not necessary.

The URL and HTML system was backwards compatible with existing protocols like FTP and Gopher. Tim Berners-Lee's original WorldWideWeb browser was able to include so-called inline graphics in HTML pages (also now known as image transclusion), but it was not untill around 1992 that other people also started implementing this in their browsers. The first popular graphical web browsers were developed: Viola and Mosaic.

15

Hypermedia Concepts

Hypermedia gives us instant access to vast amounts of information. Information items consisting of text, pictures and sound, are linked together in a network of arbitrary structure and size. These items, the nodes of the network, can be acces-sed by the user in a rapid succession. Links to related subjects can be traversed instantly. Within moments, it is possible to leap between 18th century gardening and the beginnings of life. With the potentially large amounts of information available, and the possibility of moving rapidly through the hypermedia network, one problem becomes appar-ent: How do we prevent the user from getting lost? How should the user be able to orient herself while traversing the network of nodes and links? The problem of getting lost is known as the problem of disorientation. Conklin identifies two major problems: knowing where you are in the hyper-media network, and knowing how to find some other node in the network (and knowing if such a node exists).

A basic reason for disorientation problems is that it is difficult to remember how the potentially complex hypermedia network is structured. It can also be hard to keep track of where one is in relation to the overall structure. Especially when nodes are presented one at a time only, as in for instance HyperCard, it can be difficult to remember how nodes are related and to which context a node belongs. Presenting one information item only, at a given time, can make it hard to relate items to each other, and to grasp the overall structure. Furthermore, the abstract nature of hypermedia makes it potentially more diffi-cult to comprehend than, for instance, printed media. It is difficult to directly perceive the physical volume of a hypermedia system in the same way as with a book.

Getting lost can be unproductive, even fatal, in many situations. In work situations which require quick decisions and instant action, like process control, it is an obvious risk that a disoriented operator can make serious mistakes since she does not know exactly what is going on. In learning situations, loosing track of where one is can result in frustration and negative learning effects. Confusion about how a subject area is structured and misassumptions about the relation between different topics could arise as a result of being disoriented. As a consequence the student might not only be confused, but might assimilate spurious knowledge, due to misunderstandings and misconceptions.

A central problem of hypermedia is that it might be impossible and/or intractable to know that you have seen everything of interest and not missed anything. After reading through a book, you can be relatively sure that you have read the whole material, or at the very least have an impression of how much material have been skipped. In a hypermedia system it is more difficult to be certain that you have found all relevant information. Finally, negative attitudes and dislike might arise as an additional consequence of disorientation. Getting confused repeatedly can cause negative feelings and un-necessary stress. This is important both in work situations, in learning environments, and when using information systems at museums and other public loca-tions. If the user feels uncomfortable and confused, she is likely to loose interest and discard the system.

VISUAL COMMUNICATION

In a hypermedia system, the interaction between the user and the system is based mainly on visual communication:

1. information from the system is presented on the screen,
2. the user interprets this information,
3. the user inputs information to the system, which causes the presentation on the screen to change.

Thus, the interaction is a constant exchange of messages via the display screen. Here, visual communication refer to the presentation of information in the form of text and pictures on a display screen. The term visual presentation is used to refer to the actual presentation of information. Figure 1 below illustrates the importance of visual communication.

Figure 1. Good visual communication can improve orientation.

Visualized spatial information has a potential for orienting the user that goes beyond alphanumeric messages. If information is visualized the user does not have to remember where in the hypermedia structure she is - it is shown right before her eyes. Future hypermedia systems will develop a visual language, designed to solve disorientation problems unique to hypermedia, that goes beyond that of, for example, printed media and film.

The problem of disorientation seems to arise more frequently in hypermedia than in, for instance, printed media. This is in part related to basic differences between the two media forms; hypermedia is more abstract and difficult to grasp than printed media. An additional reason is that printed media has a long tradition in communication. While graphical user interfaces have received a dramatic increase in interest during the recent years, there is still a substantial difference in sophistication between the visual communication used in even 'state of the art' user interfaces, and that of illustrated encyclopedias, magazines, and animated cartoons.

We might be able to reduce some disorientation problems of hypermedia by learning from how information is communicated in traditional media. Two important principles of communication is what to communicate and how to communicate it (which in turn depends on who we want to communicate with). Thus, we must investigate what information is needed for the user to orient herself. We will call this information orientational information. The user might for instance get lost if the present location and the structure of the hypermedia network is not known.

Furthermore, we must decide how to communicate orientational information to the user. Lexivisual presentation is a set of principles and techniques for how to present information (with text and pictures) in printed media. Central principles are: focus on the primary message, and present detailed information in the context of the whole. This can reduce the risk of loosing track of what one is reading. Often graphical techniques like zoom-boxes, miniaturized maps, and speech balloons are used. Lexivisual presentation is used in, for instance, modern encyclopedias, comic books and instruction manuals.

Hypermedia can be thought of as a visual, interactive and non-linear medium for communica-tion, which is based on a human-computer interaction paradigm where the user can browse through a database using point and click interaction techniques. Thus, a graphical user interface and direct manipulation is essential to hypermedia.

Imagine having access to a large database which contains informa-tion on a wide range of topics, like an encyclopedia. The database can contain text, pictures, animations, sound, and even video record-ings. The distinctive feature of hyper-media is the ability to browse through the material in a variety of ways. This is accomplish-ed by inserting connections between different parts of the material, linking them together. These links can be followed by the user in a very rapid fashion, using point and click interaction techniques.

Typical applications for hypermedia systems include:

— information dissemination,

— interactive encyclopaedias,

— learning, education, reference databases, interactive presentations, simulations, idea processing, writing tools, personal information management, collaboration tools, games and entertainment, like interactive fiction and adventure games.

Hypermedia is an elaborated form of hypertext. The terms 'hypertext' and 'hypermedia' were coined by Ted Nelson in the early 1970's. He envisioned a system called Xanadu, where all the literature of the world would be linked together in a gigantic world-wide distributed database. Annotations and cross-references would make it possible to browse through the literature quickly and easily. The difference between hypertext and hypermedia is that hypermedia, in addition to text, makes use of other forms of representation, like pictures, animations, and sound.

Many other researchers and computer pioneers have contributed to the evolution of hypermedia. Douglas Engelbart has made major contributions to the concepts and the technology underlying hypermedia, such as the invention of the mouse pointing device.

Nodes and Links

In hypermedia terminology, associations between different information items are called links, and the individual items are called nodes. A node can contain one or more links to other nodes, forming a network of nodes and links (figure 2). Here a hypermedia network is also called hypermedia structure.

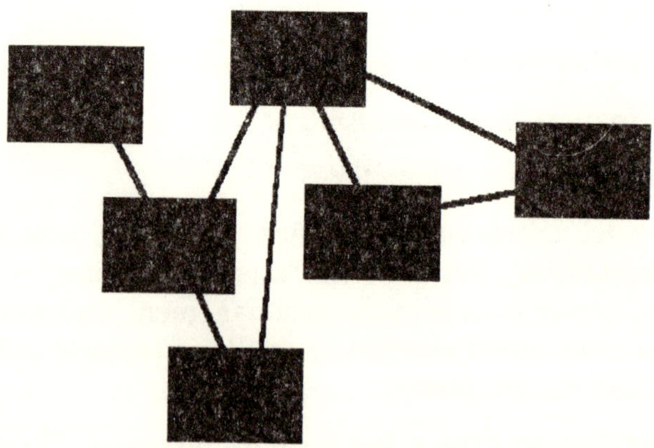

Figure 2. A hypermedia network

Nodes which contain information are related using links. Links and nodes can form a network of arbitrary structure and size. The user can move around the network in many different ways, randomly, purposefully, and so on. In this work however, we will not discuss navigation and different styles of browsing in any great detail. The ability to move quickly around the hypermedia network is critical to usability and is what makes browsing practical.

In some systems nodes are called cards. This is especially common when the metaphor of the system is based on a note cards model. Links are often called buttons. A button is an area on the screen on which the user can click to traverse a link. Nodes can be presented on the display screen in a variety of ways. One approach is to display nodes in separate, possibly overlapping, windows. NoteCards is an example of a system which uses this method. Another approach is to display one node at a time using the entire screen space. This method is used in, for instance, HyperCard. Moreover, the contents of a node might be restricted to what can fit on the physical size of the display screen, or it may contain several screens worth of information. In the latter case scrolling and panning techniques are used to access different parts of the node.

A link usually starts from a particular part of a node, for instance a word or phrase, an object in a picture, or an entire picture. The destination of a link can be a node as a whole, or a specific part of a node, like a word, a sentence, or an object in a picture. HyperCard is an example of a system in which the destination of a link always is an entire node, and Guide is an example of a system in which the destination is a specific part of a node. Links are sometimes visualized using graphical attributes like boldface text, rectangles, special symbols, et cetera.

Hypermedia and Print Media

Hypermedia differs from printed media in a number of ways. The major difference is that hypermedia is non-linear in its form. It is possible to access the material in many different ways and jump around between different information items, given that the author has provided the necessary links. While printed material, for example books, use well known design conventions, like table of contents, index, page numbers et cetera, hypermedia systems often lack such well established design elements.

The form of hypermedia systems are still experimental. Often each hypermedia author uses her own style and conven-tions. Hypermedia is also more abstract in its nature than printed media. Paper exists in the real world. In the simulated world of hypermedia it is not yet possible to physically touch and feel nodes and links.

Often a distinction is made between the author and the reader of a hypermedia structure. In some cases the user of a hypermedia system is both author and reader at the same time. Idea processing and note collecting, for instance, involves both entering information and reading that information.

Browsing and Navigation

Browsing and navigation are used frequently in the hypermedia literature. Both browsing and navigation describes the process of moving around the hypermedia network by traversing links. The navigation process aims at finding some particular information item in the database, efficiently and quickly. It is like a captain on a ship who navigates across the sea in order to reach the destination. Browsing, by contrast, is more aimless. The user can browse around a hyper-media system without any specific question or precise idea about what she looking for.

The metaphor of physically moving between nodes and links, like walking around in a city, is a common way to think about navigation in hyper-media networks. However, this model might not be suitable for all subjects. In philosophy, for instance, the material might not be straightforward to organize into a physical structure with clearly related parts. Subtle knowledge and complicated reasoning can make the traditional model of navigation unsuitable. When navigating a hypermedia network the user must be oriented.

Browsing and navigation should be contrasted to querying in database systems. When making a query in, for instance, a relational database system we have to be able to specify the question in verbal terms. Browsing and navigation does not require that we state a specific question. One of the advantages with hypermedia systems over database systems is the we can use a hypermedia system even though we have only a vague idea about what we are looking for.

When making a query to a database we can be almost certain that we have found all items in the database which contains the keywords we have entered (given that the proper keywords have been used when specifying the database). However, there is a risk that we miss information when navigating through a hyper-media system. We cannot be sure that we have seen all information of relevance until every node in the database have been examined. The possibility to specify search strings can thus be useful as a complement to navigation and browsing. Another advantage with querying is that one does not risk to get lost as easily as during browsing and navigation.

An interesting side effect of browsing and navigation is that one might come across information which would not be found otherwise. This is the same phenomenon as when we look up a word in an encyclopaedia and find additional information which catch our interest. A picture, for instance, might attract our attention to a subject we did not originally have in mind.

Hypermedia Tools

A hypermedia system consists of a database and a user interface for browsing and navigating through the database. The database contains information in the form of a model of some domain. The most common data model for implement-ing hypermedia structures is a network of nodes and links. The user interface of a hypermedia system often reflects this underlying structure in some way. Many systems use the node-link model as a basis for the user interface.

A hypermedia tool consists of an editor and optionally a high level language for creating hypermedia systems. Almost all tools place restrictions on what they can be used for. Most tools are, for example, restricted to a particular model for how information is presented on the screen. NoteCards, Hyper-Card, and ToolBook, are examples of tools for creating hypermedia systems. However, specific tools and presentation techniques can introduce additional disorientation problems.

Advantages and Disadvantages

One of the major advantages of hypermedia is the ability to quickly follow associations and look up related material. References can be traced both back-wards and forward in a way which can be difficult and time consuming with printed media. In addition, the user can annotate the material and create new references. Information can also be structured in a variety of ways. Multiple organizations of the same material allow for specialized structures for different user categories.

Hypermedia has a strong potential for learning applications since learning by exploration might be facilitated in a natural way. The student can browse the material and find new information as she explores a subject area. Concepts encountered can trigger new ideas, and chains of associations can be followed in a convenient manner. However, this is dependent of how the designer has chosen to structure the system. One approach is to have the students create their own hypermedia systems. Another possible advantage of hypermedia for learning applications is that hypermedia systems is usually considered as fun to use. Even though this might be a result of the novelty of the medium, the potential for visual richness and high degree of feedback could be regarded as positive by the users.

However, ease of browsing might increase the risk that the learner skips through the material much to hasty, and thus get a shallow and fragmented conception of the subject. An additional problem is that using a hypermedia system involves a certain cognitive overhead. The problems is that the user has to interact with the system in order to accomplish anything, which can be more or less complex.

16

Visual Communication Techniques

A number of techniques have been employed to help reduce the disorientation problems of hypermedia. The structure of a hypermedia system can be visualized in many different ways. One of the most common orientational devices is a map which visualizes the network of nodes and links. The browser used in NoteCards is one example of such a map. The basic idea of a map is to give an overall view of the structure of the database. In some systems the present location in the hypermedia structure is also indicated on the map. Figure 1 shows a typical map.

A potential drawback of the kind of maps show in figure 1 is that the graph can become extremely tangled and complex for non-trivial applications. In figure 2 this problem is illustrated. Furthermore, problems may arise when the map is not visually related to the individual pieces of information it describes.

In HyperCard it is common practice to have a map on a separate card (even though this may change with HyperCard 2.0 which allows for multiple overlapping windows). This is contradictory to the lexivisual principle of presenting related information in the same context. Since it is not possible to view the map card and another card

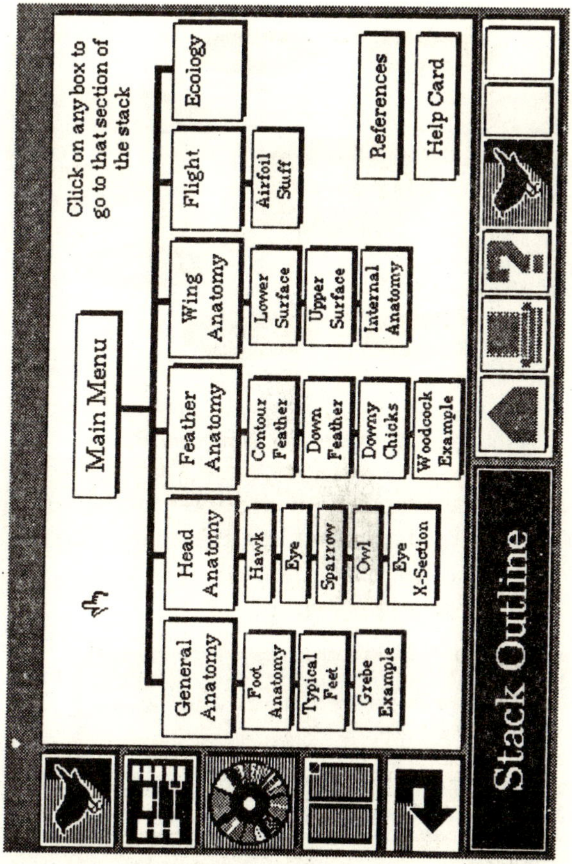

Figure 1. A map of a hypermedia network.

simultaneously, dis-orientation may arise due to the cognitive overhead of having to remember the map while viewing other cards. However, maps still provide useful information, even if shown on a separate card.

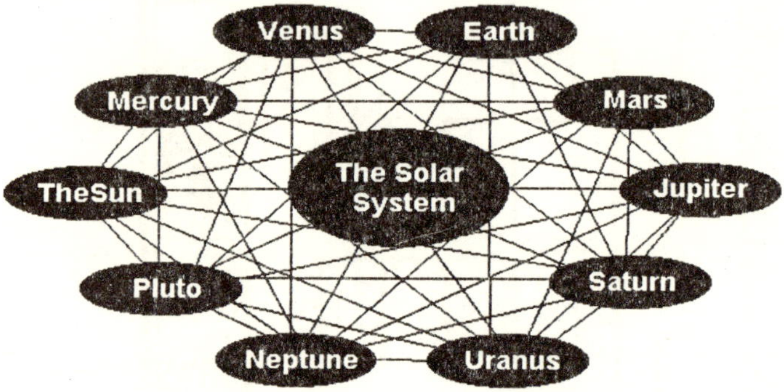

Figure 2. The problem with tangled maps

Having the map present all the time is one solution to the problem of having to remember the map. The use of ever present maps has been suggested by Kaehler. Figure 3 gives an example of such a map.

Figure 3: An ever present map in HyperCard.

In addition, maps can show information on different levels of abstraction. A problem with many maps and browsers is that they give a very abstract view of the database. Even if you are familiar with the subject, it can be difficult to relate the view provided by the map to the actual contents of the database. A concrete, pictorial view can sometimes be easier to comprehend. However, it should be noted that different ways of giving an overview are suitable for different purposes. It is not given that a pictorial view always is the best solution.

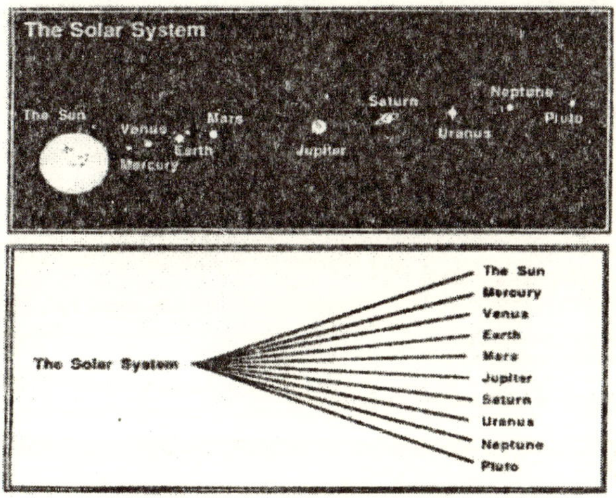

Figure 4. Abstract versus pictorial views.

Multiple Windows

Displaying nodes in multiple windows is one way to address those disorientation problems which arise from frequent flipping between different screen-sized nodes. Windows may be tiled or overlapped. The use of overlapping windows gives access to a virtually larger screen. Even if the possibility of viewing multiple nodes simultaneously has the potential of reducing disorientation problems, this approach is not without drawbacks. For example, it can be difficult to visually relate windows to each other, and thus to see to which context a node belongs. If a map is presented in a separate window it can be difficult to relate the map to the node windows. Moreover, if the number of windows is large, there is a potential risk that the display gets cluttered, which increases the risk of confusing the user. Furthermore, the burden of having to move and resize overlapping windows manually has to be taken into account.

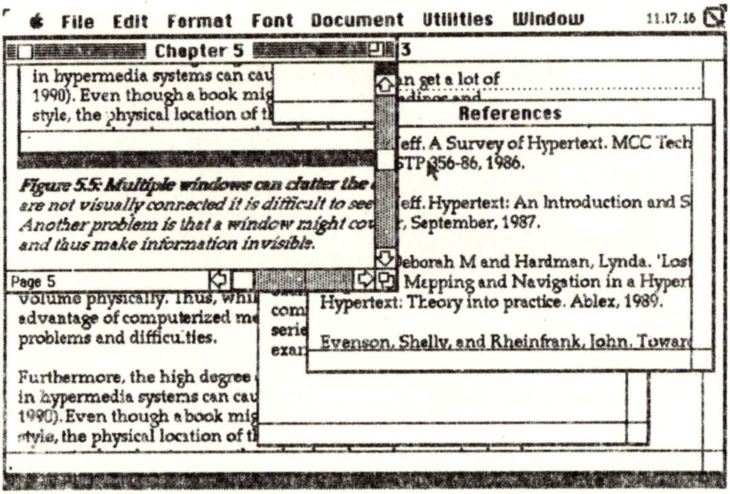

Figure 5. Multiple windows can clutter the display

One solution to the problem of relating windows to each other has been propos-ed by Reichmann, who suggests that different shades of color could be used to communicate context. Another suggestion is to use color and/or high-lighting to relate the map and the nodes to each other. Yet another suggestion is to relate the map and the nodes using arrows. Arrows can also be used to relate different nodes to each other.

Fish-eye Views

An interesting technique with respect to orientation is fish-eye views. The advantage of this kind of view is that it shows both detail and context at the same time, and thus provide a kind of world vision. The concept of fish-eye views could, for instance, be applied to NoteCards-style browsers. Moving the center of focus would then cause the browser to alter its appearance so that information close to the focus were displayed in a detailed way, while only top level nodes were shown on the periphery.

It should be noted that an optical view of the data is not necessary to take advantage of the fish-eye principle. The kind of presentation shown in figure 6 for example, has properties similar to an optical fish-eye view.

Figure 6. The fish-eye principle

Landmarks

Providing visual cues is one approach to help the user to orient herself. Points of reference can function like landmarks or lighthouses. Landmarks take advantage of the human ability to recognize information. The idea is that one should see where one is by recognizing the landmark. Thus, landmarks provide a kind of context which ties information together.

Landmarks can be in the form of easily recognizable background pictures, with one distinct background picture for each section of the database. Typographical cueing, like headings, is another example on the use of landmarks. One problem with this approach is that the meaning of the landmark, for instance a picture, might have to be learned in order to be used effectively. Therefore, it could be difficult for the new or casual user to make efficient use of landmarks. Yet another issue is standardization and consistency. Problems may arise if the same landmark is used to identify different types of information in different systems.

Techniques used in computer games are often inspired by film and animated cartoons. One example is *The Manhole,* a graphical adventure game implemented in HyperCard. What distinguishes it from other hypermedia software is the animation and cut techniques used. Animated sequences showing the movement from one place to another give a strong sense of motion. Zoom-ins and outs using animated techniques also helps to give a feeling for the present location. Moreover, carefully planned cuts between scenes provide visual continuity which help orientation significantly.

The Manhole takes place in a fantazy world of houses, rooms, and other physical places. The pictorial nature of this information makes the application of film techniques natural. A problem is that it might be difficult to apply these techniques to applications dealing with more abstract domains. An interesting observation is that people seldom have problems with knowing where to click on the screen in games like *The Manhole,* even though there are no explicit buttons. This may be because it is possible to click at almost any object. It is thus likely that something will happen if the player just tries to click somewhere. Another reason is that *The Manhole* deals with physical objects which people are used to and know how to handle. Grabbing the knob of a door, for instance, opens the door.

Yet another interesting observation with respect to adventure games, is that the player often draws a map of the rooms and the other places in the game on a piece of paper. This map is often a great help for the player. Since it is drawn on paper, and not on the display screen, it is always visible and easy to find. No obscure commands are required to activate it. It is also very easy to make quick notes.

While visual techniques are already in wide use, various aspects concerning visualization of totality and context could be improved. In a hypermedia system, as an alternative to traditional approaches, interactive comic strips with dynamic panel layout would be possible. Such a presen-tation could provide a good overview and thus enhance orientation. Figure 7 illustrates this idea.

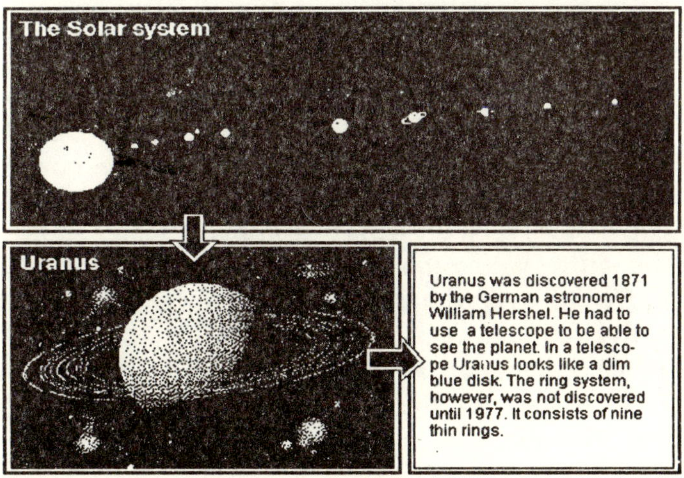

Figure 7. Interactive comics.

A page in a comic book consists of panels. The panels are usually arranged in strips, but more exotic layouts are not unusual. The advantage with panels is that they give a good overview of a sequence of events. Furthermore, balloons add dynamics and provide flow and timing to the story. However, the main advantage of the tiled panel layout is that the overview is good. The presentation shows the reading path and thus guides the reader. The sequence of panels also functions as a kind of history list; it is always easy to backtrack in the story.

A comic book provides a series of snap-shots over time, making it easier to com-prehend the story. Comic strips could thus be valuable as a complement to a film or animation. Furthermore, since no panel overlaps or covers another panel, the risk of getting confused is less than when having overlapping windows. A drawback with the comic book layout is that the tiled arrangement consumes screen space. A large screen is probably necessary for this kind of layout. In addition, panning and other browsing facilities would be necessary. One panning technique is a miniaturized map of a scrollable page with an indicator which shows which part of the page is currently visible.

It can also be difficult to develop a good algorithm for automatic panel layout. Comic pages are normally composed by professional artists who posses artistic talent and experience very difficult to automate. However, some kind of auto-matization is probably necessary, since it would be an overwhelming task to design all possible alternative layouts manually. One solution is to have the user place new panels as they are displayed, but this may cause extra work for the user. This approach is used for window placement in, for instance, NoteCards.

Interactive Pictures

An interactive picture is a visual presentation which can

respond to the user's actions. Different parts of the picture react in different ways when clicked at. This idea was originally suggested nearly twenty years ago by Ted Nelson. He proposed a variety of interactive visual presentations: hypermaps, hypergrams, queryable illustrations, and hypercomics. In figures 8, 9, and 10, an example of an interactive picture is shown.

Figure 8. An interactive picture - the basic view.

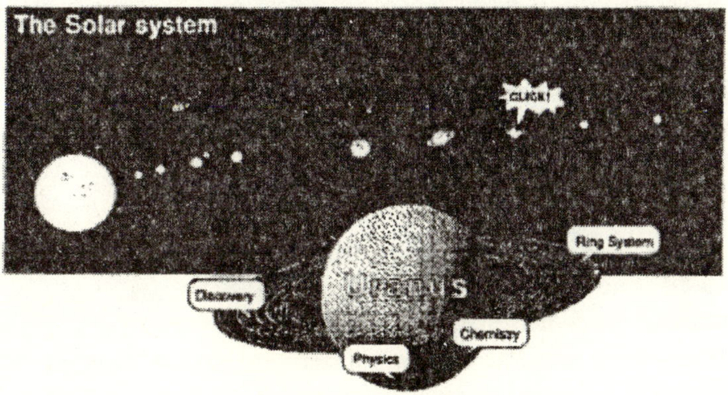

Figure 9. An interactive picture - details shown in context.

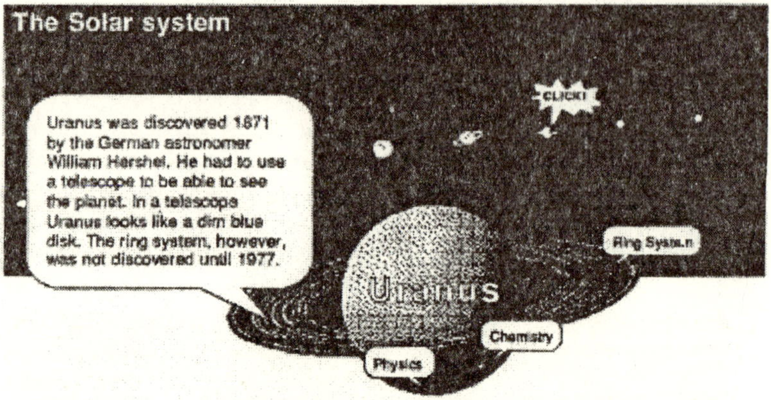

Figure 10. An interactive picture - presenting text in context.

Unlike a HyperCard stack, an interactive picture does not consist of many different cards, but of one dynamic page. In contrast to the interactive comic page, it does not consists of panels, but of interactive objects which make up the presentation. Clicking at such an object would cause the object to expand, go away, alter its shape, or animate itself. Moreover, other objects might appear or reappear, and thus alter the presentation. A typical application would be to expand and zoom in on different parts of a map, drawing or photograph. Since one is interacting with the same basic picture all the time, there is little risk of getting lost.

There is a close relationship between interactive pictures and lexivisual presen-tations. The structure of a lexivisual presentation, for instance a panel in a comic book, is very similar to that of an interactive picture. The lexivisual presentation consists of objects which are explained with zoom-ins and detailed text descriptions.

The major feature of an interactive picture is that detailed information is shown in its context. There is never a switch to another page or card. The main scene of the picture provides a visualized frame of reference for the entire presentation. In addition, interactive visuals can use screen space efficiently. This makes them suitable when screen space is limited. A difficult problem, however, is that it takes considerable skill and experience to design good graphical presentations.

An additional difficulty with interactive pictures is visualizing how much information is available. When examining an object in the real world, one can directly perceive the volume and the weight of the object. Again, the abstract nature of computer based media makes it more difficult to get an intuitive understanding of an object. Visualizations could be augmented with animation and sound, making the presentation less abstract.

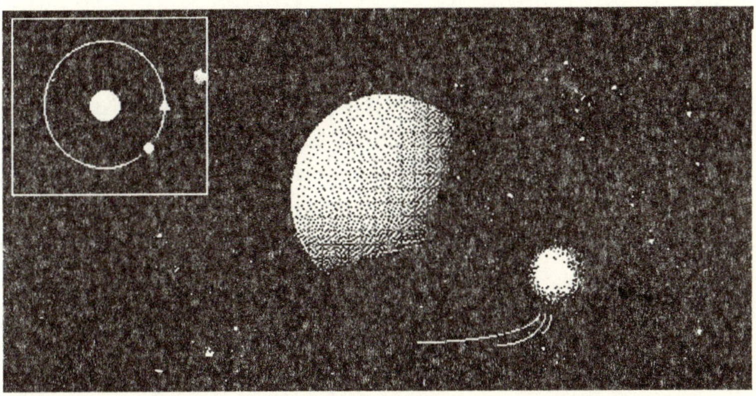

Figure 11: An interactive simulation.

An additional example of interactive pictures is interactive and animated simulations, where information change over time. A simulation would allow the user to actively influence a story, a running process, or an event. Simulations are very useful for learning purposes. Learning by doing, that is to test and explore new concepts and ideas interactively using, for instance, hypermedia based simulations can enhance the understanding. Such 'active' representations are also called enactive representations. Figure 11 gives an example of an animated simulation based on the same principles.

Interactive pictures use a model which is based on objects appearing and disappearing in the same presentation space, like actors on a theater stage. This model is also similar to that of some graphical computer games. Actually, many computer games provide the best existing examples of how interactive visuals can be used.

Object-oriented Hypermedia Tools

The tool used to implement a hypermedia system strongly influence the final design of the system. The main point of an object-oriented model is that it can make it easier to implement and think about designs like interactive pictures. While one could think of an inter-active picture in terms of nodes and links, the central idea is that instead of dividing information into small parts, one thinks in terms of a whole in which the parts (objects) fit in. This philosophy can be better supported by an object-oriented approach than by the node-link model.

The model proposed here has the following elements:

— *Objects*: Nodes as well as their contents are represented as objects. Each object can have one or more attributes. Referential links can be implemented as attributes of an object.

— *Composite objects*: An object can be a composite assembled from other objects. That is, an object can be a part of another object. This mechanism supports the displaying and hiding of groups of objects. It also supports the successive display of additional levels of detail.

— *Message passing*: Objects communicate via message passing. Sending mes-sages displays, hides, or activates objects. An object can function as a button which send messages to other, possibly composite, objects.

The notion of composite objects could help structuring the system in a less fragmented way. While the node—link model is based on a reference relation, composite objects facili-tate an inclusion relation. This allows a collection of objects to be treated as a whole. Instead of viewing the hypermedia database as a complex web, one can design systems which are structured using various abstraction mechanisms, like, for instance, hierarchy and modules.

In the solar system example each planet would be a composite object which contains additional objects for the detailed description of the planet. The whole solar system would be implemented as a composite object consisting of the Sun and its planets. One possibility would be for an object to appear as a part of different composite objects. Calvin could be such an object which appears in each of the planet descriptions. Modifications to Calvin would then appear in all descriptions.

Virtual worlds and cyberspace are receiving a growing interest by the human-computer interaction community. Both virtual worlds and cyberspace are strongly related to hypermedia. A virtual world, or virtual reality, is a computer simulated model of a real or imagined world. The key idea is to produce real-time animated simulations of rooms and other places, populated with various objects. Essential to virtual worlds is the the illusion of 3 dimensional images. One technology for this is head-mounted 3D displays which can create a vivid illusion of real space. This display technology is often used in conjunction with input devices like data-gloves and body suits. The user can move around in the simulated environment by pointing and gesturing.

Some interactive pictures and inter-active simulations could be characterized as less sophisticated virtual worlds. A video game can also be thought of as a kind of virtual world. The strong sense of a 3 dimensional space can help orientation, since we can use our experiences with orienting ourselves in the real world. A virtual world is based on an object-oriented model, which among other things facilitate presen-tation of information in a less fragmented way than the node-link model. Even though virtual worlds present objects in their proper context, disorientation is still a potential problem. It might, for instance, be dif-ficult to estimate the size and structure of the world. It can be difficult to know where in the world one is, despite the use of sophisticated output and input technologies.

Cyberspace can be thought of as a very large, distributed, and visualized hyper-media structure. Cyberspace can be conceived as an independent realm, a shared virtual environment whose inhabitants, objects, and spaces are data, but data which is visualized, heard, and perhaps touched. The virtually unlimited size of cyberspace and the heavy use of visualization techniques makes it interesting with respect to orientation. Like in a virtual world, it is important to give the user a feeling for how large the world is, where she is, and where she can go form the current location. Maps could be a helpful tool for navigating cyberspace.

The large size of cyber-space would probably make it necessary to make use of techniques like fish eye views, for example in the form of maps that use a dynamic logarithmic scale. A 3D map is also a possibility, but it is not clear how well such a device could be used. Sometimes it is much more difficult to grasp 3D presentations. For example, a 2D bar chart is easier to comprehend than a 3D one.

The multi-user nature of cyberspace (many users can populate the world simul-taneously) would make additional techniques for communicating with each other and being able to find each other necessary.

17

Visual Presentations

World vision can be provided by visualiz-ing the context of a node and how nodes are related to each other. Visualizations also help users build and main-tain a conceptual model of the system. Professional com-municators, like designers, artists, film makers, writers and illusionists, have accumulated experience of how to communicate during hundreds, even thousands of years. The art of communication has evolved ever since man started to tell each other hunting stories during the stone age.

By contrast, computer science does not have this long communica-tion tradition. It is just recently that human-computer com-munication has received wide-spread attention. Unfortunately, there has been little research on how to apply experience gained in various areas of non-computer based communication to human-computer interaction. However, it has been pointed out that such an approach could improve human-computer communication significantly.

While many other communication forms are of interest, like film and drama, lexivisual presenta-tion has several properties which are of special interest to orientation in hyper-media. As we will see soon, there are many similarities between lexivisual pre-sentation and hypermedia. Many lexivisual design principles can be directly applied to design of hyper-media systems.

Lexivisual Presentation

Lexivisual presentation is a set of principles and techniques for communicating information with text and pictures. As with all com-munication, focus on what to present and to whom is essential. Lexivisual presentation is based on the idea that associated information should be visually and spatially related, so that the reader does not have to switch back and forth between different pieces of information. This reduces the risk of loosing track of what one is reading. These are the basic principles/rules of lexivisual presentation:

— focus on the primary message

— relate detailed information to its context, that is relate details to the whole

— present related information together

— integrate text and pictures

Note the similarity between these principles and orientational information. In particular, not having to switch back and forth between isolated pieces of information could help reducing disorientation problems. Examples of lexivisual presentation can be found in magazines, newspapers, instruction manuals, and modern encyclopedias. Comics with their characteristic integration of voice balloons and pictures are excellent examples of lexivisual presentation.

In lexivisual presentation several graphical techniques are employed for communicating information in a way that gives an overview and relates detailed information to its context. Commonly employed techniques include: miniaturized maps, blow-ups, cut-away drawings, zoom arrows and voice balloons.

One of the best examples on the use of lexivisual presentation is to be found in comics. In comics, text and pictures are related using voice balloons. Comics present information in a sequence of frames, making it easy to follow the story. Orientation is easy since it is always possible to go back to earlier frames. Moreover, information is presented in its context using voice balloons and graphical symbols, like the small stars which indicates pain. The balloons make it easy to see which character is speaking. Since the reader does not have to switch back and forth between different pages, there is little risk of getting disoriented.

Interestingly, the visual language of comics is highly standardized. This is rather unique since pictures in many cases give rise to a broad variety of interpretations. Since comics readers are an increasingly large part of the modern society, it might be a good idea to use the pictorial language of comics as a basis for standardizing graphical user interfaces.

Besides the use of graphical markers like those illustrated above, comics make use of several other techniques which are interesting with respect to orientation. One distinct feature of comics is the way frames are laid out on a page. Since a full spread page is used the overview is extremely good. Authors of comics also spend considerable effort on grouping related elements of the story on each double spread page. Similar techniques could be used in hypermedia systems which use large display screens.

In addition to providing a very good overview of the action, comics employ several techniques also used in film and animation. One example is how different cut techniques are used. For example, it is common to set up the context of a scene in one frame, and present a series of close-ups in the successive frames.

18

Video Conferencing

There are many visions of videoconferencing. The essence of most of them is that videoconferencing should transcend the geographical and physical boundaries between the participants through the use of shared audio, video and other media. Ideally, a conferencing system provides the illusion that all of the participants are in the same room, sharing one space. Current products support this illusion to the extent that they provide appropriate audio, video, and multimedia communication and controls for the user.

To start thinking about how technology can be applied toward achieving this goal, consider two widely used metaphors for better communications devices - the "picture phone" and "desktop videoconferencing." The "picture phone," a telephone with video capability, has been a popular (though sometimes maligned) concept since the AT&T demonstrations in the 1960s By themselves, a pair of picture phones is limited to two participants, and only partially transcends distance and physical boundaries.

The need for a handset for sound, and the very small picture, relative to the people and surroundings, makes the participants very conscious that they are using a special device. (Use of the picture phone might be compared to use of a telescope—there is noticeable benefit, but little illusion.) In the desktop videoconferencing approach, a personal computer or workstation provides augmented audio and video. As with the picture phone, there is little attempt to mask the obvious boundaries between sites and to present an illusion of shared space. However, the augmented computer provides tremendous communication capabilities, and will be the most cost-effective approach for many users.

Depending on the application, such "multipoint" conferences may be fundamental to effective communication. To transcend the physical boundaries, first imagine an environment without the boundaries and then attempt to extend the environment beyond the normal limits. For example, try to think of "stretching" a conference room across multiple sites. First, we want audio provided in such a way to allow hands-free group discussion. Typically, this means using multiple microphones and speakers with appropriate acoustic controls.

Second, we need video cameras and large monitors to make the participants easily visible to each other. And, in many cases, we must provide for shared presentation materials, documents, marker boards, and so forth, so that most of the routine meeting facilities are shared across the multiple sites.

Similarly, imagine a classroom, or a medical practice, or a brokerage house, stretched across multiple sites. We want to provide seemingly single site facilities across multiple sites, in such a way that physical boundaries are not barriers to the participants in the activities. These metaphors, and the notion that an illusion of shared space can be achieved, set a high level of expectation of system performance. Also, we are used to the audio quality levels established by telephones and radio and the video quality levels provided by commercial television. If the conferencing equipment does not have comparable audio and video quality, the illusion will be diminished.

Achieving this performance requires real time transfer of large amounts of audio, video and data, orders of magnitude more than the quantities associated with telephones. The transfer must be directed and often must be secure, so broadcast technology associated with television is not appropriate. Thus the biggest obstacle to pervasive use of videoconferencing is the gap between the communication requirements and the limitations of the available communication infrastructure. Much of our discussion in this book is about narrowing and eliminating that gap.

Despite difficult gaps between communication requirements and capability, videoconferencing is practical and rapidly growing in popularity. Business meetings are effectively conducted by joining desks and conference rooms with videoconferencing equipment. "Distance learning" across multiple classrooms and campuses is now a routine practice. "Telemedicine" enables specialists and general practitioners to collaborate, and provides medical care in rural areas that would otherwise do without. Employers and job candidates meet without either having to travel for a face-to-face meeting. Arraignments and other legal proceedings are conducted by videoconference. Few of the participants in any of these situations have the illusion that they are located at the same sites. But many of them forget they are at multiple sites and proceed as if they were all together.

Benefits

Usually, the first benefit cited is economic. A typical business meeting of people from different locations, even a short one, can easily cost thousands of dollars for travel and lodging. There are other costs of such a meeting, such as the time the participants spend traveling, that may be much more important than the direct travel costs.

Depending on the circumstances, a videoconference may be a much more effective alternative, saving direct costs, avoiding travel time, and possibly enabling discussions that might not otherwise be possible - when travel is not possible the choices are either a teleconference or no meeting at all. It is relatively straightforward to add a person to a videoconference while it is in progress, if the person is available at any of the locations participating in the conference. In a meeting requiring travel, asking another person to join the meeting will usually not be practical.

Videoconferencing enables individuals and organizations to manage time and opportunities that would otherwise be lost. Let's take a closer look at direct costs. It is feasible to equip a conference room with a reasonable video system for roughly twenty thousand dollars. Depreciating that amount over three years, the monthly equipment cost per room can be kept to well under a thousand dollars. Costs of intra-continental long distance communication for the video systems can easily be kept well under a hundred dollars an hour. So if a room videoconferencing system is used only once a month, it will likely cost less than direct travel costs for a meeting.

These are fairly conservative figures; some users will see better cost benefits of videoconferencing. With more frequent use, the direct cost benefit clearly favors videoconferencing over travel. Similar arguments can be used to justify the costs of desktop videoconferencing systems. In this case, the cost benefit may be realized sooner, since desktop systems are much less expensive. Of course, you could say it would be more cost-effective to use telephones. But in many circumstances, telephones are insufficient. Visual contact between people may or may not be the qualitative difference that makes an activity effective.

Those who participate in multiway telephone conferences know that communication is seriously impaired without visual contact between people and shared access to documents, visual aids, diagnostic equipment, stock tickers, and so on. To help reduce these barriers, audiographics systems have been developed as a means to augment telephones with graphics such as shared documents. For some activities, audiographics may be sufficient. We believe that audiographics are a major aspect of videoconferencing, and that motion video is becoming sufficiently affordable that most applications will include video.

Cost of travel versus cost of videoconferencing is often not the correct comparison. Videoconferencing is more than just travel replacement, it is an enabler of communication that otherwise would not take place. Physical meetings are necessary from time to time, but videoconferencing users can make more electronic "trips" in a day (or week) than they can physical ones, and with much less wear and tear. The telephone is still useful, but when it is insufficient, and a physical meeting is not possible, videoconferencing technologies allow meetings that would otherwise fail, or perhaps not even be attempted.

LIMITATIONS

There are some limits that will likely not be overcome. Some individuals have a reluctance to being "on camera" and resist the new technology, just as some avoid telephones and airplanes. The boundaries between sites of a conference are visible and inhibit some activities, e.g., side conversations during a meeting, and preclude others, e.g., physical contact. As with other new technologies, estimating the extent and pace of usage growth is necessarily guesswork. Analogies to the computer industry have significant defects, but are still useful. Some have said that videoconferencing is of limited value and that few systems will be deployed.

When IBM began making computers, there were serious questions of whether more than a few tens of computers would ever be sold and used! Rapidly increasing sales of videoconferencing contradict the minimal usage predictions. At the other extreme, some suggest that videoconferencing is the next "killer application" (in the sense that computer spreadsheets were the "killer application" that spawned the personal computer market), that will drive demand for computers and communication lines. For the next few years, at least, there are sufficient obstacles to deny the "killer application" scenarios. But it is reasonable to expect growth sufficient to strain the delivery capacity of equipment suppliers and communication lines.

In the personal computer industry, Local Area Networks seemed ready for widespread usage every year from 1984 forward. Each new year was declared "The Year of the LAN." Local Area Networks became pervasive by 1989. For several years now, analysts have forecast widespread availability of videoconferencing. Some year soon, the forecasts will have become reality, without a recognizable "Year of Videoconferencing.

The technology issues that are being resolved in anticipation of the "Year of Videoconferencing." The biggest technical hurdle in videoconferencing is sending large amounts of data across existing networks that were designed for much smaller amounts. The existing networks are those intended for telephony, both local and long distance, and those intended for computer-communication, primarily internetworked Local Area Networks (LAN's). Computer-communication across wide areas typically uses the networks originally developed for telephony.

Sounds audible to humans have a frequency range up to roughly 20,000 cycles per second, or Hertz, abbreviated Hz. The sounds required for speech use a much smaller frequency range, up to roughly 3500 Hz. The telephone network is designed to transmit sounds in this smaller frequency range. Originally, this was done in terms of "analog" signals, where the strength of the signal on the telephone wires is directly analogous to the loudness of the sound, and the voltage of the signal alternates (between positive and negative) at the frequency of the sound. Most telephone service for residences and small organizations today uses the same analog conventions that were established early in the twentieth century.

Analog telephone service is not well-suited to sophisticated connections of calls, either local and long distance. Also, when analog signals are sent long distance, the quality of the signals always degrades. For these and other reasons, long distance telephone service and "private branch exchanges" (PBX) for connecting telephones within large organizations began converting to "digital" signals in the 1960's. Essentially all long distance service is digital now, as is most PBX service.

For home telephones and other phones connected directly to the telephone company switching facility, "the last mile," the circuit from the home to the switching facility, is usually still analog. The telephone uses analog signals. These are converted to and from digital signals at the switching facility. When these circuits are used for fax and computer purposes, digital information must be converted to and from analog at both ends, because the switching facility is always performing the conversion. Fax machines and computers use modems (MOdulator/ DEModulators) to perform the conversion. The maximum achievable data rate for modems using analog telephone circuits appears to be about 34,000 bits per second.

Digital representations of sounds use numbers, usually called "samples," to represent the loudness of the sound. The range of the numbers in a sample determines the signal to noise ratio. Seven bit samples are sufficient for speech, and 16 bit samples are sufficient for high-fidelity representation of music. Two samples per cycle of sound are sufficient to get good representation. Thus, for speech, roughly 8000 seven bit samples per second are enough. For music, roughly 40,000 sixteen bit samples per second are needed for high fidelity; Compact Discs use 44,000 sixteen bit samples per second, and professional recording equipment uses 48,000 sixteen bit samples per second.

Digital telephone systems are designed to handle connection and transmission of many channels of 56,000 (8000 x 7) or 64,000 (8000 x 8) bits per second, each channel representing the sounds of a telephone conversation . (In the U.S., 56,000 bit channels were used originally, but the trend worldwide is toward 64,000 bit channels.) A 64,000 bit channel is referred to as a "B-channel" (B for "bearer"). A 56,000 bit channel is "restricted." A typical telephone line in urban areas is capable of transmitting a pair of B-channels. If video is going to travel on the telephone network, it should fit within a few of these B-channels.

A picture on a television screen consists of many small dots, called "pixels" ("picture elements"). These are intended to be small enough that only the composite picture is seen, not the dots, but the pixels are readily visible if one looks closely at the screen. For North American broadcast systems, there is a maximum of roughly 360 to 400 pixels per row. There are roughly 480 visible rows broadcast, but most televisions show slightly more than half the rows. For videoconferencing (world-wide), a standard picture consists of 352 pixels horizontal resolution by 288 pixels vertical resolution. A single 352 by 288 picture is usually referred to as a "frame."

352 x 288 equals 101,376 pixels. To directly represent a full color pixel requires 24 bits (eight bits for each of the primary colors of light, red, green and blue). Thus one picture could take 101,376 x 24 = 2,433,024 bits. To have motion requires 15-30 picture frames per second, so full-color, full-motion standard resolution video could require up to 73 million bits per second, well over a thousand B-channels! Fortunately, there are bridges across this apparent chasm.

By discarding less important information (for example, using far fewer than 24 bits of color per pixel) and "coding" the information (for example, only sending the differences between frames, not the entire pictures) it is possible to send a tiny fraction of those 73 million bits and still get good results. A pair of B-channels, across a telephone circuit, gives acceptable results for many uses. With today's coding technology, six B-channels (three telephone circuits) are enough to get very good results. Using more B-channels than six, say 12 or more, allows excellent results.

The most aggressive coding techniques have led to products intended for use with modems and analog telephone lines, using about 20,000 bits per second for the video. These products use lower pixel resolution, 176 x 144 or lower, and low frame rates. These products are becoming available in 1996 as a "bundled" aspect of personal computers sold for home use, so they are likely to be present in large quantities. It is unknown how well low resolution and frame rates will be accepted for home usage. For some families, having even low quality video will be a wonderful benefit in allowing members to see each other, while for other situations the resolution and frame rate will be too limited to be considered valuable. It is not likely that low resolution and frame rates will be considered sufficient for "serious" applications.

Coding techniques can also be used to reduce the bandwidth required for audio, but not by such dramatic factors. Instead of using a full B-channel for audio, as implied earlier, it is practical to get speech quality audio in as little as one tenth of a B-channel. The primary alternative to directly using the telephone network is to use the local area networks and other networks designed for computer-communication.

The most overused phrase of 1994 was "The Information Superhighway," so we abuse the phrase a few more times to depict the bumps in that road to videoconferencing! The telephone network is based on "circuit-switching," which means that once a telephone call (or videoconference) is established, there are circuits (B-channels) dedicated to the call. Most computer networks are based on "packet-switching," which means that packets (packages) of data travel on the same network, much like boxes on a conveyor belt or on trucks on the highway.

As long as the packets flow smoothly, a computer network is a very good highway for audio and video data, providing the capacity equivalent of many B-channels. However, there are almost always traffic jams on the information highway. When the jams are minor, audio and video can get through in time and things work well. When the jams are major, conversation is halted.

Improving computer networks to manage traffic jams, and improving videoconferencing technology to mask the effects of the traffic jams, are major thrusts of current development. In 1996 there has been a plethora of products and prototypes for telephony on the Internet. As Internet telephony becomes practical and standardized, this will benefit Internet videoconferencing.

If (obviously, a "big if") adequate telephone or computer networks are available, then videoconferencing is practical for many individuals and organizations.

Videoconferencing is capable of saving travel time and money, and enables communication that otherwise would not take place.

Figure 1. Roll-about Videoconferencing System

Figure 1 shows a representative "roll-about" system circa 1996. This is a good example to start with, from which we can consider the commonality and extensions to both desktop and larger room environments. A roll-about system is a medium scale system intended for use by small groups in typical meetings. It is transportable from room to room, as long as the room has appropriate connections to telephone or local area networks.

The cabinet under the television monitor houses a personal computer and additional equipment to support conferencing. In most cases, the additional equipment is installed inside the personal computer. The camera on top of the monitor is motorized to enable convenient positioning (pan, tilt, zoom in/out) by the participants. The core technology is based on an industry standard personal computer, with added support for audio and audio coding, motion video and coding and communication protocols and interfaces. There are two major benefits of beginning with the PC.

— First, by taking advantage of the mass production and low cost of the PC, many of the conferencing functions can be provided using the PC hardware and software at relatively low cost.

— Second, the integration of the PC makes its normal capabilities directly available to the conference participants.

The television monitor is very appropriate to motion video, but has relatively few pixels per inch (roughly thirty) compared to a computer monitor (roughly 75 pixels per inch). With a group system and this relatively low resolution (pixels per inch) monitor, it is usually appropriate to devote the full monitor screen to motion video from the remote site(s). To display shared presentation materials, shared marker boards, shared computer applications, etc., either requires switching the monitor away from motion video or overlaying video with these alternate images.

For an individual, a desktop system is both more manageable in physical size and more functional. The user is usually sitting much closer to the monitor than with a group system. Rather than dedicating the full screen to motion video from a remote site, the remote site video is shown in a window, of perhaps 352 by 288 pixels out of a total of 1024 by 768 pixels. The leftover screen pixels can be used for a local site ("preview") video window, shared presentation materials, computer applications, and other images.

For a larger scale room system, two or more monitors are used to allow for display of multiple sources of video, shared presentation materials and computer applications.

APPLICATIONS OF VIDEOCONFERENCING

There are many current applications of videoconferencing

Business Meetings

Larger companies with multiple locations have videoconferencing rooms at each of their locations. They may even have videoconferencing systems in most of their conference rooms. The systems used are typically mid-scale, larger than the roll-about shown in Figure 1. The rooms and videoconferencing equipment are scheduled as part of the overall meeting scheduling. Use for intra-company meetings is probably much more prevalent than for meetings involving other companies.

One of the explanations for tending toward internal meetings is familiarity of the participants with each other. People seem to be more comfortable with using videoconferencing with people they already know than as part of a first meeting. Once companies become familiar with videoconferencing capabilities, they use it extensively. A large financial institution installed systems in two large cities 1500 miles apart. It was anticipating use in certain emergencies, with dedicated communication circuits already in place.

The systems quickly came into use six hours per day for collaboration amongst groups that had been unable to get travel funds to visit each other. One large multinational company reportedly spent $500,000 on long distance charges for videoconferencing in 1994. That figure leads to a guess that that company keeps dozens of videoconferencing facilities busy at least half the business day.

Distance Learning

Most state universities in the United States have multiple campuses, typically a primary campus and several additional campuses, and most of these have videoconferencing facilities for instructional purposes. It is often the case that a single instructor can conduct a class simultaneously across several of the campuses by videoconference. The precedent has been set for decades by broadcast lectures sent from a central site. There are obvious limitations with the broadcast approach, for example, interaction between the instructor and students, shared use of marker boards, etc.

Current videoconferencing approaches can overcome these limitations, plus provide capabilities analogous to traditional classroom facilities. For example, "student response terminals" can be used to not only give the effect of "raising hands," but also communicate specific responses. The same approaches apply outside of universities, of course, in corporate, government and other learning and training environments.

Professional Conferences

In many cases it is both of these and more. The number of conferences is both daunting and tempting for many of us because there are many more interesting conferences than we can attend. Fortunately, it is more and more common for major portions of technical conferences and similar meetings to be available, at least with audio and video, on the Internet.

Telemedicine

Medical practice is tending toward higher degrees of specialization, along with increasing numbers of general practitioners. In rural or remote areas, there may be no physicians at all. Videoconferencing is being used to allow specialists and generalists to collaborate more effectively in diagnosis and treatment, not only by allowing physicians at different sites to view a single patient, but to share radiographic and other diagnostic information and instrumentation.

Even in urban areas, it is feasible to use videoconferencing systems for patient monitoring, potentially allowing patients to remain at home. Again, it is not just motion video that would be communicated in a patient/physician visit, but diagnostic information (heart rate, blood pressure, temperature, etc.) from instruments that can be jointly managed during the visit.

Financial

There is an obvious surge toward electronic funds transfer, automated teller machines and home banking services via telephone and personal computer. On the other hand, there are still some services, for example, opening/closing accounts, loan application, and so forth, that seemingly require human intervention, possibly with more senior personnel. In many instances, these activities can be handled at a branch location via videoconferencing kiosks. In brokerage firms, traders often have a plethora of computing and information devices on their desks. One of these devices is likely to be a videoconferencing system, used for contact with other brokers, with clients and with sources of information.

Product Support

Remote support of products by telephone is routine in

many industries, covering everything from household appliances to manufacturing systems. In many cases, the customer problems are much more readily resolved if the support person can see the product and/or the customer can see visual examples from the support person. For sufficiently expensive products, manufacturers find it worthwhile to include videoconferencing equipment with the products to better enable remote support.

Legal

Some preliminary legal proceedings, such as arraignments and depositions, are handled by videoconference. The New York District Attorney's office uses desktop videoconferencing systems for arraignments. Rather than requiring the arresting officer to appear in person in court, the officer participates by videoconference, lessening travel, scheduling and other difficulties.

Employment Interviews

Travel for employment interviews is often a significant impediment for both applicant and employer, especially for initial interviews. By using videoconferences for initial interviews, the employer is able to better evaluate a pool of candidates, then have on-site interviews as warranted.

Sales Kiosks

Direct sales of many kinds of merchandise via telephone and television have been a significant trend in recent years. The customer and the salesperson often desire better communication than is achievable with a telephone call, and desire an interactivity not possible with the television shopping networks. Videoconferencing kiosks allow the centralization efficiency of telemarketing, with added communication benefits for both parties.

In short, better telephone service, better data communication, the entertainment potential of video on demand, and interactive home video are all demanding "faster, better, cheaper" communication infrastructure. The deployment trend toward pervasive, high capacity communication (the "superhighway") is likely not as rapid as predicted in the merger and partnership frenzy of 1993, but also seems inevitable. Since adequacy of communication infrastructure is the biggest issue in implementation of video conferencing, continuing improvements of the infrastructure are a major catalyst for videoconferencing.

19

Interface and Interaction Design

The interface is the intermediary between users and content, an interpreter and guide to the complexities of a site. In the graphical environment of the Web, interface design has to do with constructing visual meaning. The happy marriage of architecture and interface—of logical structure and visual meaning--creates a cohesive user experience. This marriage is crucial to helping users get around on the Web.

Subway System

Look at the example of a subway system. The Boston subway system has several routes that bisect the city, reaching a large part of the population. The subway's infrastructure is generally well planned, well labeled, consistent, and predictable. No small feat for the nation's oldest subway system, which (like many web sites) grew over time. To make the subway as easy as possible to use, its designers used color to help differentiate routes. There is a Red Line, a Green Line, a Blue Line, and so on. Cars are painted in the color of their route, to help riders make connections. Subway maps showing the various routes and their colors are prominently displayed in station stops. Walls, signs, and stairwells are also appropriately colored.

While the Boston subway system has its quirks, it's relatively easy to figure out where you need to go. Architecture (the system's logical structure) and interface (visual cues and guidance) work together to help the subway's riders make decisions and plan routes. If the subway provided visual cues that were at odds with its architecture—for example, if Red Line trains were occasionally used to service the Green Line—there would be confusion. Many web sites do the equivalent of running Red Line trains on the Green Line, though. These sites construct environments in which logical structure is not supported by visual cues.

Information Hierarchies

Hierarchies can also be visual. Visual hierarchies show relationships between elements on a page. This is done by paying attention to factors such as:

— The relative size of elements on a page

— Their placement or position

— Color and contrast

— Movement

Relative size can communicate information about the importance of one item over another. Large items will generally draw attention first and will be seen as the more important elements on screen. Headers, for example, are almost always larger than text, which communicates that they have weight and importance. When these clues are not available, sorting through information can be an overwhelming experience for users.

Placement or position of elements can also communicate their relative importance or the sequence in which we are meant to digest them. In English, we're accustomed to reading and writing from left to right and from top to bottom. The way we approach the screen is the same. Items to the left and top of center tend to be noticed first, and are usually considered more important than other items. The famous left-hand navigation panel took off partially because of its natural, comfortable location. Grouping or placing elements in proximity also provides information about their logical relationships.

Color and contrast also show relationships between items, establish importance, and most importantly draw attention. A highlight color on a page, such as yellow or red, draws the eye because of its difference from the other elements. A high-contrast black element used on a light-colored page has a similar effect. Color is also an excellent way to show a continuing path, since we can interpret color information rapidly and with a high degree of precision (yellow brick roads are as useful in life as in film). Using the full rainbow of colors without meaning or association--a common occurence on the Web—makes for poor visual hierarchies.

Movement draws our attention, an unfortunate instinctive reaction for anyone faced with a page full of eye-popping animated ads. If everything on screen is vying for attention in a Las Vegas-style glitter of color and lights, it becomes difficult to make decisions about information paths or judge relationships among content elements. Used judiciously and with purpose, animation can be an exciting and effective way to communicate information.

Rather than being seen as a solution to some of the Web's usability problems, graphic design is often regarded as their source. While they are central figures in print communication, designers are not yet playing a serious role in this medium.

The most companies are still approaching the Web with the idea that they can post a lot of marketing materials and be done with it. This approach results in

"Phase 1 sites," and adds that "most companies find out that while there is some value to this, they need to think about other concerns, especially branding, identity, and navigation. So they redo their sites. They find out that while the site may look better, be more appropriate to their company, and be easier to navigate, it doesn't do much more for them and certainly wasn't the hotbed of activity they once thought.

Because the word "interactive" has become a buzzword, confusion is understandable. "Every client is different," but we need to teach clients about what `interactivity' is most often. Web developers need to understand `interactivity' just as much as clients. Interactivity isn't about non-linear navigation or moving animations on the screen. It's about what people can do on the site, what they can participate in, what the site does to address their needs, interests, goals, and abilities."

"Developers also need to learn to build what their clients need instead of what they want to build because they think it's `cool' or fun for them. Too many sites don't reflect what a company's business is all about. They're out of character for the company. This is often a fault of the client too, but it's up to us to inform our clients of the potential mistakes they may be making. That's the value ana responsibility we bring to the relationship."

Good communication design has little to do with decoration, though it can be a thing of beauty. It's as important to a site's success as quality content, architecture planning, technical wizardry, and usability testing. When these areas come together, each presenting solutions in a unified way, each understanding the strengths of the others, the result is a well-crafted user experience

If you read much writing on design, you'll soon discover that there are many approaches to communication design. Visual hierarchies are the basic building blocks, but there are other tools available for our use. Metaphor is one of the most powerful—and most misused—of these. In the literary world, authors use metaphor to explain a concept by associating it in the reader's mind with another, more familiar concept.

For example, Yahoo-style lists of subject categories are often called "channels." This began around the time that so-called push media exploded on the scene, but these channels have nothing to do with broadcasting. They don't relate to TV either. They're misleading and misnamed, and despite having useful content, are likely to be overlooked by some visitors.

On the Web, it can be especially troublesome to play with chaos in design. For many users, the Web already represents chaos. Adding a veneer of confusion is sometimes the last straw. If scripts and animation are battling for attention, adding unreadable type and bad color contrast is probably not going to help.

What's fun and different in an MTV video or cutting-edge print magazine does not automatically translate well to the Web. If you're designing a band site or a grungy e-zine, you'll certainly have more flexibility than if you're designing a medical information site, since purpose and audience will affect the approach. But even MTV buffs deserve a structured layout. Even the nattiest hipster deserves readable text in an e-zine. Without these basic design values, you're creating art (which is about individual expression), not practicing design (which is fundamentally about communication). It's a crucial difference—especially to your users, and especially on the Web.

Things have gotten so out of hand that it's become a bit of a joke in the field (one that would be funnier if there weren't still a raging controversy over it). One site, jodi.org, uses a deliberately chaotic interface to satirize the current trend. It's purposefully confusing and makes no claims to guidance or instruction. Essentially, it's the Web's first real piece of performance art, letting visitors experience what chaos in interface design feels like.

In navigation design, it's cruel and unusual punishment to offer chaos instead of guidance, self-expression instead of shared communication. Interface design, like many areas of design, is service-oriented--it's in service to the message, the client, the users, and the medium. That makes the work of an interface designer a serious challenge, since it is much harder to understand others' needs than it is to know your own tastes. There may not always be glory in it, but service is the hallmark of good design.

In Visual Explanations, Tufte explains that shuttle engineers knew the night before the launch that there was the possibility for disaster. A critical part, a seal called an O-ring, was not expected to work correctly in the extreme cold forecast for the morning of the launch. Navigating the Web could hardly be called a matter of life and death (though cases of fatal misinformation exist).

Good architects tend to understand what this is all about, and some of our finest public buildings and corporate workspaces are the tangible results. Information architects understand that this same concept can be applied to information spaces. Design is not a battle between form and function, emotion and reason, decoration and purpose. In your users' eyes, these elements are intertwined, for better or for worse.

It's virtually impossible to separate the design process from end users, readers, or visitors. They're the reason we bother with visual messages in the first place. Without these users, you may as well be broadcasting into deep space. Understanding human quirks is as much a part of a designer's toolbox as high-end graphics software or a good set of drawing tools. If anything, it's more important.

On the Web, where we're shaping new and sometimes experimental interactive spaces, these issues are thrown into high relief. It's essential that we try to understand how people are likely to react to problems, why they sometimes fear the screen, and how they learn new things. Without understanding some of these areas, predicting the active process of navigation becomes little more than guesswork. Without understanding some of these areas, we'll never get past our reputation as an unfriendly and butt-ugly medium.

If you accept that a web site is a space, then it's natural to assume that there are objects in it—things we can pick up, manipulate, press, or otherwise interact with. There may be control panels with buttons to press, or drop-down menus to scroll through, or objects that change when you roll your mouse over them. All of this may end up sounding a lot like building a transistor radio—and in a way, it is.

Principles of Good Design

— *Visibility.* By looking, the user can tell the state of the device and the alternatives for action.

— *A good conceptual model.* The designer provides a good conceptual model for the user, with consistency in the presentation of operations and results and coherent, consistent system image.

— *Good mappings.* It is possible to determine the relationships between actions and results, between the controls and their effects, and between the system state and what is visible.

— *Feedback.* The user receives full and continuous feedback about the results of actions.

Paying attention to these user-centered design principles—visibility, conceptual models, mapping, and feedback—is not just for designing phones and transistor radios. Think of how many times you've clicked on something believing it to be a link, or gone to a page that offered no feedback about location. These are important design principles, whether it's industrial design or navigation design.

Interactivity

Interactivity has become a bit of a buzzword. Interaction, in a nutshell, is two or more people having an exchange—of ideas, of emotions, of physical objects, of words. On the computer, interaction is still two or more people having an exchange, with the exception that the interaction is mediated by technology. Interactions on the computer are often as complex as interactions off the computer, and it's helpful to understand both.

Politeness is one essential ingredient of a positive interaction. We know this is true in daily life, but surprisingly, it seems to be true in computing situations as well. When media violate social norms, such as by being impolite, the media are not viewed as technologically deficient, a problem to be resolved with a better central processing unit. Rather, when a technology (or a person) violates a politeness rule, the violation is viewed as social incompetence and it is offensive.

20

Computer Literacy

Computer literacy usually consists of "an understanding of uses, advantages and limitations of computers" or computer literacy means "developing skills to use computer applications which bear on persistent life situations such as communications, education, governance, consumerism, entertainment, and employment. A general overview of the majority of work in computer literacy shows a number of "universal" understandings for computer literacy programs. These include:

— A knowledge of computer theory, including some knowledge of how computer hardware makes possible and constrains the things a computer can accomplish.

— Learning hexadecimal and binary number systems.

— knowledge of algorithms and data structures, where "one who is truly computer literate must be able to 'do computing' - to conceptualize problems algorithmically, to represent them in the syntax of a computer language,... and to express computational ideas clearly... and with a high degree of organization and readability. These skills are said to provide the basis of an "educationally sound preparation for the information age".

— A knowledge of the history and development of computers.

— A knowledge of what a computer is and what it is capable of doing.

— Some programming ability, usually in BASIC, Pascal or Logo. This is usually characterized as a lesson in "structured thinking" which the student is supposed to get from exposure to programming.

— The ability to apply computer skills to information retrieval and communication in the process of problem solving, and decision making. This includes the ability to use computers to access information that is unavailable or difficult to access via other means.

— The ability to choose software and applications in support of some defined objective. Includes the ability to distinguish between applications that suit one's needs and ones that don't.

— The ability to apply computer skills and tools to the problems of everyday life at work and in the home. Here, computer literacy means "the ability to process information in support of the decision-making process".

— An understanding of the "social impact of computers", by which some mean that computers are sometimes used to "steal money and information" and that computers have both positive and negative social impacts.

— The ability to control a program and a computer to achieve a variety of personal, academic, and professional goals.

The length of the David Johnson et. al. list notwithstanding, no one author has done a thorough job of defining the term computer literacy. Perhaps Albert

Goldberg has it right when he says that terms like computer literacy "mean whatever one wants them to mean, applied to whatever educational environment one works in, institutional or otherwise".

What all of these definitions have in common is that none of them incorporates any critical understanding that moves beyond computers themselves. What critical understanding there is - calling for an appreciation of the "ethical and legal implications of computer usage"- never challenges the assumption that computers are part of the solution and not part of the problem. Additionally, many of these definitions are completely focussed on computer technology and ignore the goals and objectives of the people involved. They assume that computers are amoral, benign devices, something to be known objectively.

In general, their view of computer literacy is one that glorifies computers. It is one that exhorts computer literacy programs to train entry-level computer operators. It is not one that would produce students who are critical of the activities in which they are engaged. In short, for the majority of the educational press, computer literacy is simply the ability to deal with the computer itself in terms that it understands. Any other uses for computers grow out of and are incidental to these skills.

There is a sharp contrast between the clarity of the goals and means to those ends when educational authors talk about the technical-rational part of computer literacy and when they are discussing the socio-political actions and consequences of computers. The discussion is quite sharp, with little in the way of ambiguity, when these authors are discussing how computer language training should take place. Completely the opposite is true when they begin talking about how students should come to understand the impact(s) of computers in society.

All these definitions are both right in some senses and completely wrong at the same time. They are correct in that, given that it is highly unlikely that computers will somehow disappear from society, everyone should know something about them, even if they do not own one or even expect to do so. On the other hand these definitions are seriously problematic because they are basically technologically determinist. This view of computer literacy as focussed on the applications end of the use of computers is not, as has been noted, one pole of the argument, offset by a different view of computer literacy as programming ability.

It is rather, the logical progression of the development of the idea as those who sought to define the concept tried to keep pace with the developments in the computer field itself. By the mid-1980's, definitions of computer literacy came to focus more and more on the abilities of users to extend themselves into the world at large with the help of a computer. Computer literacy was no longer defined as just the ability to write programs and understand how computers themselves work. The definition was being expanded to include the ability to pick a proper software applications package, modify it if necessary (although not necessarily by modifying the code internally) and put it to work to solve problems. In one sense, the notion of computer literacy was being expanded to include the "degree of competence required to function in today's world". Note that this extension is not away from computer-centered activities.

There is no mention of using computers to exchange information the way that books are used to build a bridge for ideas across time and space. These definitions see the computer and its applications packages as the central organizing tool. What these definitions of computer literacy fail to note is that a computer is a tool that places constraints on the work being done by virtue of the kinds of problems it is capable of addressing and "solving."

In Another side — there are a variety of arguments posed against those touting the value of computers in society and of computer literacy to individuals. Rather than directly debating the points of the computer proponents' arguments themselves, these arguments tend to focus on examining the underlying assumptions of the proponents of computer literacy. They ask deeper, more critical questions of computers, their use and potential.

The core of these arguments is that, in society's willingness to computerize, or perhaps more properly in society's seeming indifference to the computerization of every possible aspect of daily life and social interaction, society is concomitantly impoverishing itself in the education of its children, deluding itself about the necessity and value of computers in general, wasting its money on computer literacy programs that will not advance individuals or society in any kind of reasonable, useful way, and empowering the military, computer and pharmaceutical industries.

Given the instrumental goals that seem to pervade most of the notions of computer literacy, these points deserve careful consideration. Much of this criticism asks why educators are so eager to jump uncritically on the computer literacy bandwagon. The critics of computer literacy accuse educators of buying into the notion that computers are an inexorable condition of the future and accepting the concomitant notion that the majority of the population have no control over shaping this force.

The deeper criticism that is offered in answer is that there seems to be little conflict between the widely accepted goals of education - the development of "concrete-operational skills of technical reason coupled with functional, utilitarian language skills" - and computer use - cost cutting in educational institutions by the institutionalization of the computer as deus ex machina, coming to solve the difficulties education faces, usually through CAI activities instead of human teachers.

Computer systems foster and abet a mechanistic kind of thinking that "has been exceedingly powerful in our uncovering and coming to understand the mechanical, physical cause-and-effect dimensions of reality" but is not adequate to the job of understanding the whole of the reality of a given problem or issue. By introducing computers to children at an ever-earlier age, we are setting ourselves up for a mechanistic, bland and colorless world in the future. Education has emphasized the development of technical-analytical skills for quite some time now, and the introduction and proliferation of computers in the classroom only exacerbates the trend.

Students and workers need to be able to use computer technology in schools and the workplace, the others need to know computers to be effective as consumers and citizens. For the first two of these groups - students and computers - Noble argues that computer literacy is necessary for some of the people in each of these groups but not for the vast majority. What computer literacy really means for those people who do need it, is going to be determined by the specifics of the situations where they find themselves.

People can learn whatever they need or want to about computers [as the need arises and without] having to be prepared or "literate" beforehand. The idea of computer literacy as preparation for later application, seen, for example, in comparisons between computer literacy and music appreciation, fits nicely within a "basic-skill" mentality that refuses to allow that fundamental knowledge is best acquired in the process of useful activity, not beforehand in useless introduction".

For the second two groups, consumers and citizens, no computer literacy is really necessary at all. Given the power that the market exerts in the daily lives of people in the US, if someone has something to sell and it necessitates the use of a computer to sell it, someone will create a software and hardware package that makes it possible to sell that product to the functionally illiterate. Another aim of the critics is to demonstrate that the pursuit of computer literacy reinforces the hegemony of the status quo. The main thrust of this argument is that by creating a computer-literate populace, in the manner conceptualized in the current discussion of the term, that populace would be more inclined to accept the idea that technological solutions to the problems of society are the way to go.

In other words, a computer-oriented society is one in which the high-tech imperatives of the military-industrial complex take precedence and those imperatives are unlikely to be questioned. Noble notes that many people - educators, merchants of computer machinery, politicians, parents, journalists, etc. - seem to be behind the idea of some kind of universal computer literacy. He makes the point that much of the argument about computer literacy centers around the idea that it is somehow implicit in the maintenance of America's superiority in the world technological marketplace.

In terms of the value of computer literacy, much of the rhetoric about jobs and skills just doesn't hold up under close examination. The vast numbers of jobs that computers are supposed to create for the "post-industrial" society simply do not exist. If anything, computers eliminated many jobs and degraded the required intelligence needed to perform many others. As for those people who expect to see more jobs in the future, based on the introduction of computers in new fields, Noble notes that they are guilty of falsely equating the superficial kinds of skills gained in computer literacy programs with the highly technical kinds of knowledge necessary for taking what jobs there will be in computerized industries.

This will be even more true as time passes. Advances in software and hardware are making even simple programming skills less and less necessary for the average computer user and therefore for computer literacy programs as well - but no one seems to have told this to the computer literacy program designers and journal writers who seem stuck in the late-1970s. The ease of use of the newer systems, coupled with a burgeoning software industry that seems to be willing to produce any conceivable kind of program, has all but eliminated low-level programming needs and skills - why would anyone wish to go to the trouble to write a program that can be bought for a few dollars and comes with a guarantee?

Finally, with the exploding popularity of the Apple Macintosh and like computers and software, the time it takes to become familiar enough with a machine to make beginning use of it has dropped from days to hours, perhaps minutes. Yet, there has been no discernible change in the agenda of the educators pushing the mainstream views of computer literacy. In fact their views have not so much changed as remained the same. Proponents of computer literacy still talk about which language students should know and how best to train people so that they can pick the proper application for a given job.

Newspaper Coverage of Computer Literacy

The one place where the notion of computer literacy is most problematic is in the newspaper press. What coverage there is in the newspapers focuses mostly on specific classroom settings and specific computer programs, Computer Aided Instruction and grand expectations about future implications of computer use in education. In the newspaper coverage, definitions of the term "computer literacy" are more often than not, not given. When definitions are provided, they are superficial and work toward revealing more about the assumptions of the writer than they do toward expanding the readers' understanding of the term.

Although the term computer literacy was being widely debated in the educational press in the late 1970s, it isn't until the early 1980s that it is even used in the mainstream newspaper press - in the Los Angeles Times in 1981 and in The New York Times in 1982. Nowhere in the newspapers surveyed was the meaning of the term debated. It is difficult to tell which is more striking, the lack of definition and argument about the term computer literacy, or the assumptions that the education writers for newspapers make about their readers. When computer literacy is defined in an article, it is usually defined as "acquainting students with computers and teaching them to program the machines" or "the skills necessary to get an entry-level job in the data processing industry".

Frequently the definition takes on some of the instrumental flavor found in the educational press: "Interviews with students, teachers, principals and others disclose that most schools use computers mainly to teach computer literacy - teaching about computers themselves". This kind of analysis (if it can be called that) resonates nicely with the objectives of the developmental theorists of the educational press. Here is a popular presentation of computer literacy that echoes the idea that computers are built and used in a vacuum. Given that there is no critical examination of the term in the newspapers, it should come as no surprise that there is little development of what the term might mean as well.

If the term computer literacy is not clearly defined, the applications of computers in the classroom are, at times, more clear. The virtues of Computer Assisted Instruction (CAI), roundly debated in the educational press, are as taken for granted as the definition of computer literacy. Here, the notion of computers and CAI as the deus ex machina of education is strong. One examination of computer assisted instruction notes that computers are wonderful devices that "are completely and perfectly consistent". This notion is coupled with the idea that computers are "colorblind" and do not discriminate in the basis of race or ethnicity.

The conclusion therefore is that computers are impartial teachers. However no mention is made of the not-so-colorblind distribution of computing resources in inner-city schools. Nor does much of the newspaper or educational press mention that the dryest, most instrumental CAI programs are the least expensive and most likely to be in poorer school districts while the wealthier schools get the less instrumental, more interesting and newer programs. Only the dullest, rote-drill programs are found in the poorest districts - those poor districts which can afford computers.

This return to CAI in the newspapers is just in time for the "Back to Basics" educational movement resurfacing in the rhetoric of the George Bush 1990s. A feature article that praises CAI as the best way to put computers to use in the schools has nothing but praise for a program that drills students in reading skills, noting that the use of computers and CAI raised the students in Calvert County's Sunderland Elementary School District from 12th in the state to 3rd in terms of their California Achievement Test scores between the 1980-81 and 1986-87 academic years. This program focuses on "basic skills," but the author doesn't define the term, and has helped "boost 83 percent of the students above the CAT's 50th percentile".

In the 16 years of newspapers surveyed there was one article that warned: "if your local likes to brag about its PC population and how computers are 'an integral part of the classroom learning environment,' get yourselves down there and find out just what that means.... For most students, real education from classroom computing is a hoax". On balance with the educational press, this kind of critical appraisal is about par. In the newspapers' coverage of the issue of computers in schools, they are overwhelmingly on the side of the development side of the debate. One thing is clear from reading the newspapers.

Writers in the newspapers don't read or follow the arguments in the educational press, not even the "education" reporters. If reporters paid more attention to the "serious" press then they would be contributing more to popular understanding of computers. Then the might leave themselves less open to the kinds of criticism which notes that: Coverage of the computer-literacy movement in general has been characterized by a less blatant but more insidious variety of an approach that allows for a debate, but effectively keeps it within narrowly established limits. The truly difficult questions about whether or not the nations classrooms should be computerized are neatly finessed. Instead, discussion is limited to how this process should take place.

Given the ways in which the press regulates itself, its claims to "objectivity" and "balance" it's not surprisingly there is very little in the way of press critical to computer use in the schools. Instead, as Menosky notes above, what there is is the sense that computer literacy and computers themselves are a necessary change, necessary to maintain the technological superiority of the US in the world:

The wholesale introduction of computers into classrooms since 1980 amounts to a quiet revolution that will help meet the demands of scientific and technological change as well as economic competition in world markets. A decade from now American students... will have a real advantage in their technical and higher reasoning skills. Compared with their counterparts in other countries, they will be better prepared for competition in a world economy.

If this sounds familiar, it should. It is precisely the same line of rhetoric voiced by Deringer and Molnar above and resonates in tune with the Education Czars of the Reagan and Bush administrations. From this admittedly narrow survey it would appear that there isn't much interest in discussing definitions of computer literacy or discussing the use of computers in education much beyond specific settings. This lack of interest in the newspapers keeps their writers from contributing much to our understanding of the term. Apparently it also keeps them from developing their own understanding of what computer literacy and computer use might be as well.

If one looks through the newspapers, it is difficult to find much in the way of critical thinking about the issue of computer literacy and computer education. Just as there are occasional articles that take a critical stance on computer literacy, so to are there articles which see computer literacy in more than the traditional, instrumental ways. One article which does this, interestingly enough, is from 1981, and defines computer literacy in terms that have to do with computer retrieval of information in a library setting.

Critical-Functionalist Views

In opposition to the dominant view of computer literacy explored above, one that takes the technology as given and asks the student to learn how to accept it uncritically. This argument about the place of computers and computer literacy in education not include the two most popular elements from the discussion of computer literacy elaborated above, i.e., programming and applications.

For the first, learning to program only serves those who have particular needs, most notably the defense industry. Few individuals ever find a need to write programs for their own use. Employers will hire highly-skilled programmers to write the code they need and there will not be all that many jobs for programmers. There will be even fewer jobs for people with some knowledge of programming, despite trade school claims to the contrary. For almost all users and needs, there are and will be a selection of already-prepared applications programs available from commercial sources. Programming for the private citizen then gets reduced to the level of a hobby. Anyone that interested in programming can and will learn how to program without having to be taught how to do so as an integral part of their formal education.

And for the other question - having the ability to chose between applications to get the one that best matches the job at hand, this is a non-issue. Most people, with the exception of high-level bureaucrats in large commercial concerns and government agencies, will chose applications like they chose automobiles (and the differences between applications are about as distinct). They will ask their friends, they will "test drive" the package and sometimes they will make mistakes. Just as no one is arguing that people should learn about the internal workings of automobiles before they buy a car neither should we worry about learning to chose between Lotus and Excel.

Developmental modernizationalist are, at bottom, the wrong way to conceive of computer literacy. They take the technology as given, as inflexible and as a tool for "serious" work like mathematics and accounting. They tend to ignore the fact that most of the population has little need for any of the functions they ascribe to computers. A computer would only make the job more thorough.

In addition, these theorists fail to see that the kinds of activities that would make people more able to define their own lives are precisely the opposite of the kinds of activities they have outlined for computer literacy courses. The computer program that teaches individual critical reasoning skills has yet to be written and probably never will be. The skills that come with learning to program and to run a spread sheet are extremely valuable for anyone going into business and wishing to make a profit or for figuring out what kind of business one might go into. But those skills are of little use when it comes to figuring out whether or not the business is something that society really needs.

In other words, computers are useful for establishing certain kinds of goals, and for figuring out how to reach a predetermined goal. They are of much less use in asking or answering the philosophical, value-laden questions that one needs to explore in setting those goals, particularly in modern society where such goals are all too often set without any examination of the larger value questions. This argument will take an entirely different tack. It argues that what is important is learning to use computers as a medium of communication so that those users can participate in electronic discussions. These discussions are already taking place on a multitude of private bulletin board systems and numerous commercial ones as well. In addition there are new technological developments in data transmission on the horizon that will bring even more opportunities into people's homes and lives.

Computers and Competency

Scholarship, citizenship and political activity, if the last can be thought of as separate from the first two, are all communal activities. Despite what appears to be the prevailing ideology, e.g. that individuals are all-important and sole causal agents in the creation of their own realities, people still feel the need for interacting with their communities, however this last is construed. The critics of mass-society theorists notwithstanding, there is more than a little truth to the criticism that modern mass media push people away from political and social interaction with each other and into atomized spaces. The result of this is the creation and maintenance of the illusion that individuals are the powerful, causal agents of their own destiny and that cooperative, collective social action is somehow an activity of the "lunatic" fringe.

Computers too have their aspects that push people off by themselves. Computer games, playing with numbers, shopping services, keeping accounts and the like, all are activities that allow individuals to keep to themselves in a private, individualized space. But computers, unlike most of the earlier electronic and visual media (with the exceptions of photography and, more recently video) allow for interactive participation with other people via the medium. The mass media of the late 19th century and present - radio, phonography, film and television - allow the audience to sit and watch or listen.

What discussion there might be about the content of the medium, takes place elsewhere, either in newspapers and magazines in the form of criticism or around living rooms, in restaurants etc., where people gather to talk about the films, television and music they've heard or seen. In computer-mediated arenas, the primary effect of participation is interaction. Rather than more or less passively accepting what's on the tube, the participants create what's on the tube. The participation in a computerized activity of discussion requires two things: technical competency, what would normally be subsumed under traditional definitions of computer literacy, and some motivation to participate in discussion with others. What follows here is a discussion of the first: technical competence.

The definition of technical competency proposed here is the practice of learning enough about computer-based technology in non-specific ways so that the individual can engage in activities that bring him or her into contact with other people to discuss, argue, and coordinate activities that are outside the use of the computer itself. This does not imply or demand knowledge of particular computer operating systems, software or computer languages. It is rather, the acquisition of an indeterminate set of skills which allow the user to hack his or her way through encounters with new technology.

This kind of competency comes from several sources. First is the opportunity to work with a variety of computers and applications. In the world of the 1990s this means some experience with both Macintosh and IBM/MS-DOS operating systems. This does not mean a thorough knowledge of either system, just knowing the basics of each so that when either is encountered the user can do more than just stare helplessly at the screen. Part of this knowledge is knowledge of at least one word processing software package. Which package doesn't matter. What is being sought is a sense of the kinds of things that word processing software is capable of doing, what kinds of tools are provided as part of a word processing package and what they allow the user to do.

For instance all word processors allow the author to create text, to delete and change words and lines of words and to move lines, paragraphs and sections around in the body of the text. Once a user understands these few basic ideas they will begin to build a set of expectations about word processing software, expectations that they will carry to their next encounter with a new package and which encourages them to experiment with that new package to get it to perform up to their needs. This sense of expectation and experimentation is central to the entire notion of technical competency being proposed here. The same sense can and needs to be acquired through exposure to some kind of distributed system like USENET, PEACENET or The Source. Here what the user should acquire is some sense of what kinds of things an electronic mail system or bulletin-board system usually provides.

Electronic mail systems usually allow the user to read and send mail, to store and retrieve old mail and to integrate a word processor with the mail program so that they can create and edit their outgoing mail. Most programs allow the user to forward received mail to other users as well. Most bulletin board systems allow participants to read and post messages in the public space of the system and many allow electronic mail along side of the public discussion space. Once again, tools learned in one computer-mediated environment will be expected in another and, when they are not found, the user is likely to either ask that they be provided or to hack together some substitute from what tools are available on that system.

The kind of competency suggested here goes deeper into the psychology of the individual than just encountering computer hardware and software and acquiring some facile mastery. It is the coming to understand the mindset of technological competence, a mindset that views any technology as ultimately understandable. Additionally, one cannot put a technology to use successfully if one does not understand that technology and is therefore limited to making use of it in ways predetermined by others.

This kind of understanding is being acquired by the current generation of children. For those people who are over 25 years old or so, micro-computers are something that came along after they were into their teenage years or later. For the children who were growing up in the 1980s, microcomputers are part of almost every human-made object with more than two parts they encounter. For them programming a VCR or dishwasher poses little in the way of a threat. And, for them, moving to computers will pose little in the way of the technophobia that characterized the first computer interactions of their parents. Computer literacy should then be the process of building a critical understanding of both the technology and the world, on top of that technical competence.

Having separated the ability to manipulate technology from the notion of computer literacy, it is time to talk about a new formulation of the notion of computer literacy. The view here is that computer literacy is the practice of making use of computer technology to find out and act on the information that computers make available. This view relies on the idea that computers are useful for holding discussions wherein the participants can come to know their own voice and where they can use that voice to make sense of their own history. The framework for this conceptualization of computer literacy comes from an interpretation of the work of Paolo Freire. Freire's notion of literacy is one that sees literate practice as a way of taking hold of the world one lives in and, through the process of naming the objects in that world, taking hold of that world as well. This argument centers on the use of the computer to enact an elaborated version of Freire's notion.

According to Freire, finding and speaking one's own voice in the act of naming the world is an act of profound political empowerment. It is an act of empowerment because it implies that some people do not sit passively while others make the decisions that affect their lives, those who speak are those who decide. In Freire's view, everyone has and should be permitted to speak and be heard. Implicit in this process is some forum for speaking. In the modern world, those platforms are sadly lacking. Computers and the information services they allow access to are one place where new platforms are opening up. This means that computer literacy is the ability to make use of computer technology for investigation of the world, and coordination and disagreement with others. Finding and using ones' voice ala Freire, Heath and Vasquez, implies the ability and opportunity to engage in the interpretation and reinterpretation of texts with others as a way of engaging in political action.

History exists in two places - in books and in peoples' minds. Freire talks about history as useful for shaping individual lives if that history is part of and relevant to the lives of the people who attempt to mobilize it. The importance of these notions of history and its usefulness for the practice of computer literacy as defined here is that the discussions this notion of computer literacy calls for would afford people the opportunity to come to understand their history in new ways that lie outside the history of William's "selective tradition" - history as recorded by others in books.

Part of learning one's own voice is learning what Macedo calls a "'language of possibility' [which enables] learners to recognize and understand their voices within a multitude of discourses in which they must deal". Essentially what Freire and Macedo are calling for is a political plurality, in which the speaker learns both to distinguish his or her own voice and in which the speaker learns to respect the voices of others. What this activity requires is some place where one can put one's own voice in debate with others. The activities that take place on computer bulletin board systems and in other computer-mediated environments are an excellent place to experiment with and develop a voice.

One of the interesting things about computer interaction in a well-distributed system is that anyone who participates will soon find themselves with both supporters and detractors. Posting political opinions, no matter how mild, almost always insures a response from both sides of the issue. The response of one's "friends" gives one the courage to continue and the criticisms of the others adds impetus to sharpen one's arguments.

If one takes the example of reading and writing words as the archetype literacy - literacy in its most basic sense - then computer literacy needs to be seen in its relation to reading and writing and the equally important relation between reading, writing and the creation and transmission of information. Computer literacy then, comes to encompass as well the ability to make use of computer technology to understand, store, retrieve and manipulate information, coupled with a critical understanding of the particular medium itself. Computer literacy, like general literacy, should not be thought of as a specific set of skills which allow the student to read and write at some imagined level - i.e. the "sixth-grade level". Computer literacy is part of a process of opening a "writable" window on the world.

21

Social Interaction and Groups in Text-based Systems

Social interaction and groups in text-based systems have a longer history. There are four major groups—(1) identity, (2) social order and control, (3) community structure and dynamics, and (4) collective action.

Identity

All of our interactions, even those with strangers, are shaped by our sense of with whom we are interacting. In face-to-face and telephone interactions there are a wealth of cues of varying reliability to indicate our identity and our intentions. Our clothes, voices, bodies, and gestures signal messages about status, power, and group membership.

Online interaction strips away many of the cues and signs that are part of face-to-face interaction. This poverty of signals is both a limitation and a resource, making certain kinds of interaction more difficult but also providing room to play with one's identity. The resulting ambiguity over identity has been a source of inspiration to many who believe that because people's physical appearance is not manifest online (yet), individuals will be judged by the merit of their ideas, rather than by their gender, race, class, or age. But others argue that traditional status hierarchies and inequalities are reproduced in online interaction and perhaps are even magnified.

Deception can bring great benefits, but deception is useful only if some members of a community honestly signal what sort of person they are. A signal that is used deceptively by an entire population carries no information. Donath thus asks what maintains the balance between honest and deceptive signaling, and makes the point that some signals are inherently difficult to mimic.

A signal is inherently reliable to the extent that it is more costly for mimics to emit than it is for those who actually possess the quality. A classic example is conspicuous consumption as a signal of wealth. A person of limited financial means will find it very difficult to display the chauffeur driven-limousine, mansion, and other signals of wealth. To take an example from the Internet, one's proficiency as a programmer can be signaled by included an example of one's work in a Usenet posting. Indeed, there is a convention in the Usenet newsgroup alt.hackers of including a clever hack in each post to establish one's identity as a skilled hacker and to keep out impostors. Signals that are to some degree inherently reliable are called assessment signals. This is in contrast to conventional signals which have no necessary connection to the trait they advertise (e.g., simply stating one is wealthy or a skilled programmer).

Knowledgeable members of the Internet realize that each domain name has its own reputation and recognize the different implications of commercial versus institutional accounts. The content of the post contains its own set of signals about the identity of the author. The writing style, the facts that are brought forth, the proper use of abbreviations and argot that are specific to the group, all help establish or challenge the user's identity.

At the end of each post is a signature which has also become an important element in establishing an identity.

Signatures are a combination of business cards and bumper stickers that members use to display their interests, opinions, and occupation. By providing the address of one's company and position, the signature can help establish one's credentials and create the possibility of accountability (one can check the company to verify the information). Donath also provides a number of fascinating examples of the use of codes or esoteric knowledge as a way of establishing one's identity. Another common element that is now seen in signatures is the address to the author's web page. The simple link to a web page is significant in a number of ways.

The fact that an elaborate set of web pages represent a substantial investment of time and effort may also have the effect of encouraging identity persistence - throwing away an alias used in previous postings may be a trivial act, but dismantling a set of web pages and constructing a new set may involve costs that the author is not willing to bear. There is yet another source of identity information: the author's history of previous posts on the Internet. Interaction on the Net leaves a trace of varying durability. Posts to Usenet discussion groups can usually be accessed for a few weeks and some groups maintain archives of past discussion. The search for the traces of someone's past interactions has changed radically in recent years with the development of extremely powerful search engines and durable, extensive databases.

An early promise of online interaction was that it would render irrelevant such markers as race, gender, status, and age. Because online interaction strips away physical markers, the assumption was that social categories assumed to rest on physical characteristics would wither away. In online interaction racial identity springs from a participant's perspective on racial issues rather than from physical cues. The reliance on a participant's written words as a source of racial identity also reverses the usual sequence in stereotyping.

In online interaction, an individual's beliefs and attitudes are used to make inferences about the individual's race, rather than the more familiar route of inferring attitudes based on physical racial cues. While any racial identity might be claimed in this textual world, this does not guarantee that others in the group will acknowledge or support the claimed identity. Racial identity is interactionally negotiated - people do not create racial identities by themselves and the identity portrayed in a posting might be accepted or vigorously contested by other members in the group.

Sometimes a group member will attempt to cast the poster in another identity as a way of challenging the poster's arguments. This is a common method of challenging a person, and that arguments often center around what identity a poster can reasonably claim rather than directly challenging a poster's arguments and views. The structure of the Usenet also makes it a useful research site for studying the dynamics of group boundaries. Because messages can easily be crossposted to other groups, the audience for a discussion can rapidly expand or contract, drawing in other groups with different identities at stake.

Conservatism of Cyberspace

The most optimistic proponents of the Internet have argued that gender, race, and age become unimportant in online interaction. At the very least, many assume that the absence of these markers will provide the opportunity to explore and invent alternate identities. Jodi O'Brien sharply contests this view in her chapter on *Writing in the Body:Gender (Re)Production in Online Interaction*. O'Brien argues that gender is such a central feature for organizing interpersonal relations that persons go to great pains to reproduce gender in online interaction. "Are you male or female?" is such a commonly asked question that it was long ago abbreviated to "RUMorF?" Significantly, no such abbreviations are in widespread use for questions concerning age, height, weight, socio-economic status, etc. Gender is the one characteristic of our embodied lives that is a central feature in interaction throughout the Internet.

And it is not simply that gender is reintroduced in a world without physical markers. O'Brien makes the striking point that gender is reintroduced in a more limited and stereotypical manner than exists in embodied interaction. There are no limitations to how one might describe oneself in cyberspace. Yet the gender descriptions one encounters on the Internet show far less variation and imagination than occurs in face-to-face interaction. People recreate themselves as stereotypical ideals, and O'Brien points out that this "hyper-gendering" is especially prevalent among those who attempt to "cross-dress," (i.e. males presenting themselves as females). The implication is that a world without constraints has led to greater homogeneity rather than new forms of identity.

The attention given to the possibility that someone might be gender-switching points out the crucial importance of gender identity in cyberspace. The fear is that a close friend or the object of one's seduction is not "really" the gender they present themselves as. The debate as to whether and when gender-switching is appropriate has led to a vocabulary of motives that makes crossing acceptable as a way of avoiding harassment or experimenting with a new perspective, but inappropriate if there is an intent to "deceive." This is hardly a clear line, and one person's experimentation is another person's deceit.

There is a deeper tension. O'Brien points out that there is strain between those who view online interaction as an opportunity to "perform" a variety of perhaps fabricated roles versus those who see cyberspace as a new communication medium between "real people." O'Brien argues that the distinction between the intent to "be" and the intent to "perform" may be much more useful than discussions about what is real versus non-real, or honest versus deceitful. She concludes that "the most contested issue at the moment in the history of online communication may be how to establish ways of underscoring real versus fictitious sites so that users can reliably distinguish 'real authenticity' from 'authentic fantasy'."

Thus, the issue is clearly signaling the frame of the interaction so that individuals know whether this is a site having more to do with theater (and therefore authentic and consistent fabrication, as is true in many role-playing MUDs), versus a site where identity is tied is some reliable way to one's "real-world" embodied self (as would be necessary for legal and financial transactions).

Social order and Control

Social organizations vary in terms of the amount of control, coordination, and ultimately the coercion they can exercise over themselves. Social control rests in large part on a group's ability to identify individuals in order to hold them responsible. Building on identity, we look at the nascent institutions of self regulation and governance in online groups.

A range of power structures that have emerged in cyberspace. It is widely believed and hoped that the ease of communicating and interacting online will lead to a flourishing of democratic institutions, heralding a new and vital arena of public discourse. But to date, most online groups have the structure of either an anarchy or a dictatorship. Some notable experiments with democratic electoral politics have failed dramatically, raising questions about what sort of governance is possible and what the prerequisites are for democratic institutions. Several different approaches to social order are examined, including public punishment, ostracism, and mediation.

First Age of Social Control

Despite the utopian hopes of early settlers, it became clear very quickly that some form of monitoring and sanctioning would be necessary in online groups. "The failure of the ideal of complete freedom in cyberspace was an early phenomenon." So begins the chapter by Elizabeth Reid on *Hierarchy and Power: Social Control in Cyberspace*. Reid examines the dynamics of power and methods of social control in two kinds of MUDs: Adventure MUDs and Social MUDs. In Adventure MUDs, users participate in role-playing games which involve scoring and strict hierarchies. The structure of the games requires a serious commitment to the community for the reason that one must play the game frequently in order to collect the resources necessary to keep one's character "alive."

Social MUDs, in contrast, involve more free-form interaction and the ability to build new objects in the world. It is possible to participate in Social MUDs much less frequently than in Adventure MUDs because one's character continues to exist over time without the need to explicitly find food, shelter, etc..., as is the case in the role-playing Adventure MUDs. In common with many other forms of online interaction, the relative anonymity and lack of physical contact that is a feature of MUDs encourages users to become less inhibited. This is not to say that members of MUDs exist in an anomic state. Reid rightly points out that there is "no moment on a MUD in which users are not enmeshed within a web of social rules and expectations."

The disinhibition that is common in MUDs can encourage the formation of intimate relationships and deep feelings of attachment to other users. The other edge of this dynamic, however, is that members of MUDs can act out in a hostile and violent way without the usual fears of retribution. While it is true that threats of physical violence in online interaction are almost always empty threats, there is the possibility to do great symbolic violence. Tales of online harassment and "rape" are already well known, and Reid adds a particularly striking example of virtual violence involving a MUD dedicated to the support of persons who have experience sexual assault.

Reid uses the community's response to this crisis as well as examples from other social and adventure MUDs to describe a variety of methods for social control. Some forms of social control require the intervention of the owner of the MUD or one of the high ranking "wizards" who can control and rewrite the software that underlies the MUD. Other methods come from the members themselves, acting either singly or in concert with others. Among the possible forms of social control that are brought up in Reid's discussion are the following:

Eliminating commands in the system that chronically lead to objectionable behavior. An example is the decision by the owner of the MUD mentioned above to eliminate the "shout" command in that community.

Providing commands that allow members to filter out objectionable behavior. "Gag" commands, which are available in many communities, allow users to ignore what a particular person is saying and doing. However, as Reid discusses, there are important limitations to this technique. Some communities also allow its members to intentionally select what actions to which they wish to expose themselves. In some adventure MUDs, one can choose to open oneself up to the risk of having one's character killed, or alternately to prohibit this kind of attack on oneself.

Temporarily restricting the rights of transgressors. A member might have their movements restricted or lose the right to use certain commands for a period of time.

Shaming and humiliating a transgressor in public rituals. The owner or wizard of a MUD can force a transgressor into a public space, strip away their abilities and perhaps allow other members to shame and ridicule the person.

Banishing a transgressor from the community. A wizard can also force a transgressor out of a community, although the ease with which one can acquire another account and identity on the Internet means that a determined person might find a way back into the community.

Instituting stricter criteria for admission to the community. To try to avoid problems to begin with, some communities restrict membership, imposing a limit on the total number of users, for example, or requiring that new members be sponsored by existing members. Other communities prohibit guest visitors or severely restrict their abilities.

Increasing accountability by registering identities. Some communities require that members have one, persistent identity as a way of increasing accountability. Other communities also require members to register their legal names and phone numbers with the head of the community.

Regulatory committees. Some MUDs have experimented with regulatory boards composed of members to oversee, for example, the construction projects of the community's members

Moral Entrepreneurs and Vigilante Groups. Of course, individual members can take it upon themselves to express their dissatisfaction with the behavior of another. In some cases, groups of members can even band together in order to try to right some perceived wrong. In some adventure MUDs, for example, posses are formed to hunt down and punish users who have killed other users. There have also been incidents in which groups have brought in a "hired gun" to punish another member.

Reid makes the provocative point that the emphasis in many MUDs on public punishment, humiliation, and ostracism marks a return to the medieval in terms of the technology of punishment. The body of the users - albeit a virtual body - is once again the site for punishment.

Institutionalized Mediation

Anna DuVal Smith discusses a very different source of social control. In her chapter on *Problems of Conflict Management in Virtual Communities,* she documents the emergence of institutionalized mediation in one community. Online communities, Smith observes, are distinguished from many face-to-face communities by their open boundaries (users can enter and leave the MUD with much lower costs than physically moving to a new community), the relative anonymity of computer-mediated interaction, and the possibility of great social diversity (members may come from many different countries or ethnic groups, and may have very different expectations about what the goals of the community are). Each of these features can encourage conflict. Smith argues this means that methods of conflict resolution may be both more important and more of a challenge than in many face-to-face settings.

Research in dispute resolution has identified three basic routes for conflict resolution:

— exercising power,

— reconciling interests, and

— adjudicating rights.

Drawing on her experience in dispute resolution in face-to-face communities, Smith introduced mediation and fact-finding procedures into the MUD in which she was a member. The catalyst for these reforms was an episode in which the wizards of this MUD intervened to punish a member by using the technical powers at their command to banish the member and destroy the objects he had created in the MUD. Their response was widely seen as inappropriate and illegitimate by many members and led to a series of reforms aimed at trying to better manage conflict. The community decided to (1) severely limit the abilities of visitors to the community, (2) to require sponsorship by two mentors and (3) a period of socialization prior to full membership, and (4) to provide a dispute resolution process.

The mediator's role was made more difficult by the fact that users connecting from different time zones made it difficult to schedule meetings. Lag in the network, and the fact that some members had to deal with much more severe lag than others, also meant that it was very difficult for some users to participate. There was also the problem that evidence (such as email logs) could be falsified. On the other hand, the same disinhibition that may have provoked the conflict to begin with also encouraged members to be forthcoming with facts and details about an episode. The absence of physical cues also had some positive consequences, making it easier, for example, to overcome the barriers of socio-economic differences. Even network lag had a positive side in that it provided time for thought and reflection before reacting.

Smith concludes that the conflict resolution methods that were introduced to the community were useful. The Advisory Board of the community agreed and institutionalized the mediation procedures. Nevertheless, she cautions that there are significant challenges to establishing and maintaining a system of mediation.

Members must be aware that a mediation procedure exists and believe it is a fair and legitimate process. A second challenge is that cases can take quite a long time to resolve. Finally, there is the simple fact that members of the community who are both skilled and willing to invest substantial time and effort must staff the process. A system for resolving disputes is a public good, and there is the temptation to free ride on the efforts of others.

Structure and Dynamics of Online Communities

Cyberspace is already the home of thousands of groups of people who meet to share information, discuss mutual interests, play games, and carry out business. Some of these groups are both large and well developed, but critics argue that these groups do not constitute real communities. Something is missing, they argue, that makes these online groups pale substitutes for more traditional face-to-face communities. Others respond that not only are online communities real communities, they also have the potential to support face-to-face communities and help hold local communities together. Opinion rather than analysis and evidence characterizes much of this debate, and surprising little is know about the actual structure and dynamics of online groups.

Online communities surely differ in important ways from face-to-face communities - that is a premise of this volume. But when contrasts between online and face-to-face communities are made, especially if these contrast have a moral character, it is imperative that we be clear what the comparison point is. When, for example, critics describe online communities as more isolated than "real-life" groups, their comparison seems to be to an ideal of community rather than to face-to-face communities as they are actually lived. There is a great deal of loneliness in the lives of many city dwellers.

Community is now conceptualized not in terms of physical proximity but in terms of social networks. Telephones, automobiles, and airplanes have long meant that it was possible to establish and sustain important social relationships outside of one's immediate physical neighborhood.

Visualizing Social Cyberspaces

In William Gibson's now famous vision, cyberspace is "A consensual hallucination experienced daily by billions of legitimate operators, in every nation ... A graphic representation of data abstracted from the banks of every computer in the human system. Unthinkable complexity. Lines of light ranged in the nonspace of the mind, clusters and constellations of data. Like city lights, receding."

In practice, however, the landscape of the Net has been difficult to see. There is no single unified representation of cyberspace or even of its major components. The tools used to connect to social cyberspaces leave us blind to a range of information that is otherwise visible in face-to-face interaction - information such as who is in the room, where they are located and clustered together, what the room is like and what expectations for behavior it signals. In online interaction the experience is something like attending a cocktail party and only being able to see people who are actively speaking, while the room and all the listeners are invisible.

In Invisible Crowds in Cyberspace: Mapping the Social Structure of the Usenet, Marc Smith explores a method for generating maps of the social networks created in the Usenet. Smith proposes a research agenda in which long term historical studies of large-scale social network can be carried out. His goal is to create a series of maps showing what different regions of social activity look like. Smith discusses a range of measurements that can be generated from a collection of data from the Usenet news feed.

Relationships between groups - in particular through a practice called crossposting that links groups together through shared messages - can be visualized as networks and then contrasted with other groups. The Usenet is examined in terms of the distribution of activity and diversity of participants. Smith proposes to use these measures to develop a classification system for online groups. What his research makes clear is that cyberspace is not homogeneous. The Usenet newsgroups he studies are as varied as any set of face-to-face social groups and spaces.

Smith highlights the range of methodological and ethical issues raised by research conducted in this manner. The maps created by this project reveal in great detail a social space that had previously been cloaked by the unwieldy nature of the data. Many people have a high expectation of privacy in computer-mediated interaction despite the fact that they interact in what can be seen as a public space. But new technical tools change and shift the nature of this space. Smith explores the implications of these tools and data for researchers interested in developing further studies based on records of interactions in cyberspace.

Anyone who has spent time online has probably experienced aggressive, flaming responses from someone. The hostility that exists on the Internet is a common and oft-repeated complaint. In fact, it is common to find individuals who are remarkably generous with their time and expertise. Howard Rheingold has even described the interactions within one online community as a gift economy. Kollock takes this metaphor as his starting point and examines the structure of gift-giving and whether that is an appropriate model for online interaction.

He argues that much online interaction is characterized by a form of exchange that is both more generous and riskier than gift-giving. Many of the favors and benefits provided in online communities are public goods, i.e., a good from which all may benefit, regardless of whether one has helped create the good. In such a situation there is a temptation to free-ride on the efforts of others, but if all do so, everyone is worse off. Kollock argues that the economies involved in producing many public goods change radically as one moves to an online environment.

The costs of communicating and coordinating the actions of a group, for example, are often much lower than in face-to-face interaction. And the value of a piece of information or advice that is offered to a group can be amplified because of the fact that this is a realm of digital information in which an unlimited number of people might use or make copies of the information provided. It is also the case that the size of the group necessary to produce many public goods is often reduced to one. This is to say that single individuals are capable of producing and distributing valuable goods or services to a huge audience on the Internet.

Collective Action

Communities rarely exist exclusively in cyberspace. It is important to investigate the ways in which social groups in cyberspace spill out into the "real" world and vice versa. Social protest, the linking together of rural communities, and collective action by a disadvantaged community are examined.

Dynamics of Online Social Protest

The effectiveness of the Internet as a tool for coordination and communication can be seen in the success of social protests that were carried out online. Particularly striking was the critical response to MarketPlace - a CD-ROM that was to contain information about 120 million American consumers - and the Clipper chip, an encryption technology that provided a "backdoor" to be used by the government as a form of wiretapping.

Online interaction permits individuals to mobilize far more quickly, cheaply, and efficiently than is usually possible. Relevant information can be posted publicly or forwarded to particular individuals or groups at little or no cost. Significantly, it is also relatively easy for individuals to find other individuals with similar concerns and interests. The fact that specialized discussion groups brought people of similar interests together meant that participants were likely to share many assumptions and concerns, which would facilitate communication within the group.

Yet these same features can also be problematic. The speed and range of communication can encourage the spread of inaccurate information, and the common ethos shared by many of the participants can discourage challenges to the information and conclusions of the group. The specialized nature of the discussion groups can become too insular and force out dissenting voices.

22

Computers in Society

Most users of personal computers today work with several kinds of computer programs that are called collectively applications software. There are three main positive reasons why people turn to them for a variety of applications: (1) making a job more economical (savings of time or money) or more convenient; (2) making feasible a job that is impossible to do by any other method; and (3) using the computer to gain insight into a process by modeling or simulating it. These three reasons for computing make the machine a powerful tool in all areas of modern life. The three often overlap in both common and exotic applications, and it is hard to find applications in which at least one does not fit. The computer has become a positive force in most areas of life because of its characteristics: its flexibility, generality, speed, and accuracy. Some years ago, they are still relevant to current computer usage. Following are the major four major fields of application today: education, medicine an d science, the media, and government.

Users ordinarily choose them to increase their productivity in doing day-to-day work; consequently, these applications programs are also called productivity software. Whereas formerly packages carried out single functions, nowadays they are often bundled together in a multifunctional package that can share data among functions. Such software, called an integrated package, usually includes word processing, spreadsheets, and database capacity. Most people adopt applications software for economy and convenience, but both feasibility and insight often have a place in its use. The five most common types of application are word processing, spreadsheets, database packages, graphics, and communications.

Word processing is using a computer like a typewriter, to prepare documents, but it offers far more flexibility than typing. Even basic word processors make revision and editing easier than on a typewriter. And they offer features which were never envisioned for typewriters, such as the ability to elect different character fonts, stylistic options, and spelling checking. Some modern word processors even have typesetting capabilities that allow the user to do desktop publishing. They are now certainly more than substitutes for typewriters, and offer ease of use and features for document preparation never before feasible with personal computers.

Spreadsheets are analogous to automated accounting sheets, numerical figures laid out in rows and columns. The spreadsheet's advantage over manual accounting techniques is that it can do calculations automatically and update the ledger immediately. Suppose you are making a budget for the month and do not want to spend more than a quarter of your assets for housing. Your spreadsheet would have a slot for income and another for housing expenses, to be calculated at no more than one fourth of income. If you have put the formulaic relationship between income and housing into the spreadsheet, adjustments to income trigger the software to recalculate new housing figures conveniently and quickly. As you enter different income figures, the computer automatically refigures the housing budget to reflect the quarter-of-income allowance for that purpose. Ease of planning and insight into the budget process contribute to the popularity of spreadsheets.

In principle, database and file management packages are analogous to manual filing systems, such as an index card file for a mailing list of 5000 contributors to a charity campaign. The card file is probably organized alphabetically by the last names of the people on the list. Also included on each name card is other associated information, such as the contributor's address, broken down into street, city, state, and ZIP code; the amount of the contribution; and the number of years the person has been giving. If the list of givers is very long, reordering the index card file to pull out all people in a certain ZIP code area who have contributed over $100 in the last three years would be tiresome and troublesome. However, when the information is put into a file management program, a one-file database of contributors, the process of sorting and searching becomes easy, for the application provides these functions as standard features. Most database packages can handle multiple files and interrelate them for powerful control over large amounts of information. Simple searches for ZIP codes, although not impossible with a set of index cards, are convenient and economical with a file management package. In addition, complex searches like the one proposed, a kind of computing for insight, become feasible.

Computer graphics packages allow the user to treat the computer screen as a drawing pallet and then print the results in black and white or color. They are commonly used either for creation of freeform art and design or for graphing numerical information. More complex graphics programs for computer-aided design (CAD) allow engineers to model building plans and machine tool designs directly on their screens. Today artists are using graphics packages to design logos for companies and lay out advertising copy, often in conjunction with desktop publishing packages with word processing features. Since it is often said that a picture is worth a thousand words, people regularly choose to graph their numerical or financial data to make them easier to understand -- an aspect of computing for insight. Creation of line and bar graphs and pie charts are often standard graphic options in spreadsheet programs.

The increasing popularity of the Internet in recent years has led some commentators to suggest that the latest "killer app," jargon for an innovative, widely adopted computer application that makes some person or business rich and famous, will be software for data communications, such as Web browsing tools. Yet data communications covers a wide variety of useful applications linking computers and the telephone system. Equipped with a modem, hardware that changes computer signals into telephone signal's and vice versa, a home computer user can access information from a variety of public and private sources or send messages throughout the world. Using the phone connection to check airline schedules and reserve tickets at home can save time and money. For a doctor seeking medical advice for an unusual condition, quick access to remote medical databases may make feasible the saving of a patient's life. Electronic mail, the sending of a message to another person's "mailbox" on another computer, and computer conferencing, multiple users commenting by electronic mail on an issue of common interest, offer extended two-way transfers of information and provide insight not readily feasible by other means.

Popular acceptance of these common kinds of applications software has been the major reason why the personal computer has been so successful. The machines that run the packages are reasonably priced; the ease of use and adaptability of their software have spurred microcomputer sales in all fields. Indeed, all areas of the professions, business, and government have incorporated these tools for a multitude of common and unusual tasks. The combination of productivity software, microcomputers, and general users represents a successful instance of the Computer Triangle. The result has been the burgeoning personal computer revolution throughout the world.

Computer Use in Education

Applications software like word processing and the increasing presence of the Internet represent only a sample of common computer uses found at all levels of education from kindergarten to college. Innovative strategies in computer-assisted instruction (CAI) include student multimedia projects, simulations in history and science, and electronic mail between students geographically dispersed throughout the world. Yet questions and debates still persist about the methods and quality of incorporating computers in education.

Pedagogical issues: No one questions that computing in education is a big business. According to the Software Publishers Association, roughly $2.4 billion was spent on educational technology in public schools (kindergarten through grade 12) in 1994, and IBM Academic Consulting estimates more than $6 billion for college and university purchases in the same year.

The traditional lecture method of delivery, with students sitting passively in a classroom, is giving way to networked classes and the teacher's becoming more of a mentor to guide student exploration of a topic. Students can communicate with each other through class networks and do team projects in a variety of multimedia (Reinhardt). Proponents of these digital, computer technologies in education argue that they make instruction more vivid and fitted to individual student needs.

In addition, administrators and public officials often believe that computers will lessen the spiraling costs of education. A study at the University of Southern California reported in 1995 that fewer than 5 percent of college faculty members were using computers in instruction to enrich learning. Many teachers, trained in the lecture mode of instruction, report that they do not have the time to invest in learning new technology. They are skeptical of the benefits that the new modes of delivery will make in the education of their students. In many institutions personal commitments of faculty to educational computing do not lead to tenure or promotion. And faculty are even more suspicious of administrators' arguments for cost savings coming from technology.

Joseph Weizenbaum, long a leader in educational technology at MIT, has been a longtime critic of hastily adopted educational technology. He warns that people should not expect computers to replace the most valuable relationship in the educational process, the human contact between teacher and student. Weizenbaum thinks that going to the library and reading a novel about the Great Depression is better than gleaning loads of facts and statistics about it from a database. A multimedia database on the Depression contains an anonymous someone's selective gathering of information about a complex period, while a novel like James Farrell's Studs Lonigan provides a capsule reading of real life.

Teachers should try to foster a student's natural talent for imagination and hold on to it as long as possible. Weizenbaum certainly agrees with much educational research that computers should be used carefully in conjunction with well-planned classroom teaching (Brady). Few would argue that computers can replace a good teacher. But they can provide hard-to-teach supplemental dimensions or demonstrate with other methods. In the successful cases, the three elements of the Computer

Triangle—hardware, software, and people—are working together for better education.

Computer Assisted Instruction

Much use of computer-assisted instruction in schools involves drill-and-practice software. These are programs designed to teach a particular kind of knowledge and to drill students for mastery. Some of this software is especially appealing to young learners, because it incorporates color graphics and sound feedback. Programs to teach the phonics approach to reading fit into this category, along with foreign language and mathematics drills and supplementary lessons for remedial students.

As students get older, drill-and-practice software tends to become boring and lose its appeal, unless it is cleverly designed to hold their interest. A multimedia program in American history called Point of View (Scholastic Software) uses a mixture of timelines on politics and popular culture, census statistics, and recorded sound to overcome the element of boredom. It takes students' interest in this important subject and their probable lack of knowledge about parts of it as a point of departure for their investigations. Students can follow their individual preferences in working through the program's materials.

For instance, students can choose to display several different historical timelines at the same time. As they view the dates of important rock music events in the pop culture of the 1960s, they can also display the political events of the Kennedy-Johnson era, including the civil rights struggle and the Vietnam War. They can play recorded excerpts of important speeches, such as Kennedy's inaugural ("Ask not what your country can do for you") or Martin Luther King's "I have a dream" speech, from the March on Washington. The possibilities for graphing census statistics are extremely varied. Students can choose to graph the numbers of white and black residents in several states. As they move through several decades on the timeline, the graphs are automatically updated and displayed on the screen. Students can save materials from the package to use in developing their own research papers with word processing programs. The package intentionally embodies a flexible, interactive learning environment to encourage students to develop their own research strategies and to learn more about American history than their textbooks contain.

Multipurpose Computing

Creative teachers at all levels of education have always found ways to incorporate innovative teaching aids and strategies in their classes. Computers add new capabilities not available by other means. One positive example is the "computer-infused classroom" in a middle school in Shoreham, New York. There a creative teacher, Robert Vlahakis, includes three computing components in an American history course: simulation, telecommunication, and standard software packages (Vlahakis).

Using data communications software, Vlahakis's students correspond with peers in other schools by electronic mail and extract stories from a public on-line news service about current events related to class materials. They are learning how to gather and use information, a skill that will be more important than memorization of facts in the next century, when massive databases on all subjects will be accessible from computer keyboards. With their word processors and desktop publishing software, students work in teams to prepare their own newspapers of important historical periods. They gather textual and pictorial materials, type or scan them into the computer, and compose newspapers such as the Jamestown Memo or the Plymouth Bay Sun for the

Revolutionary period. For them the computer has made American history come alive.

Simulation software also provides these students with insight into the historical process which they experience vicariously. Having to make decisions based on the available evidence shows students that the answers to real world problems are usually open ended. It forces them to use higher-level thinking skills, like logic and deduction, to solve a problem. Shoreham students use a simulation package called *The Other Side* (Tom Snyder Productions) to negotiate a peace between two nations, and they rate the experience a highlight of the course. To Vlahakis, "Computers have added another dimension to the teaching style that I have always employed—an experiential, problem-solving approach that encourages students to question, discuss, and analyze history. The computer has made it more efficient for me to focus on the individual needs of my students in a more diversified learning environment." All three of the positive reasons for computing are involved in this class: efficiency, insight, and the feasibility of trying individual teaching strategies not available in other ways.

Teachers report that simulations are especially useful in teaching mathematics and science. Mathematics is hard to teach partially because many complex functions are difficult for students to visualize. The highly respected mathematical package called Mathematica (Wolfram Research) overcomes this problem (Grady). It can carry out almost any kind of mathematical operation—numerical, symbolic, or graphical. Math educators are beginning to rethink their assignments to catch up with Mathematica's potential to enliven the teaching of mathematics, especially for college students.

In the experimental sciences, educational simulations often meet several needs. Perhaps the subject is hard to understand without experiment, or unsafe for students to experiment with in real life, such as infectious disease. The high cost of equipment required for an experiment may preclude having it available for student use. Sometimes a simulation cuts out a long delay in waiting for a reaction, or shows something impossible to observe, such as what happens at the atomic level (Trollip). Simulation packages in mechanics, electromagnetism, and modern physics, produced at Stanford by Blas Cabrera, present animated results on the computer screen so that students can visualize not only the processes in progress but the final result.

Computers in Medicine and Science

Accurate information and speedy access to it are probably more important in medicine than in most fields, given the life-and-death situations that doctors and nurses face every day. Medical databases of current research findings and treatments, well indexed by categories, were one of the first major uses of on-line databases. In Computers and the Information Society, James Radlow tells the story of a California doctor in the 1980s who was able to save the life of a patient with uncontrolled bleeding by tapping into MEDLINE, a well-known medical database, from his home in the middle of the night. Among summaries of 19 articles on this type of bleeding, he found an English translation of a German case which seemed to match his patient's symptoms and described a new blood replacement therapy. The doctor ordered the treatment to begin immediately and found the patient much better in the morning. Access to knowledge through data communications and up-to-date on-line medical databases saved the patient's life.

Today "telemedicine networks" allow specialists in large medical centers to do diagnosis at long distance through computerized two-way videoconferencing, using high-speed data communications. Small towns have access to the knowledge of big-city physicians on-line, whereas they could never afford to have such doctors in their communities. For instance, in May 1994, a woman in rural Georgia had a rotting skin lesion on her leg that was not responding to treatment by local doctors. Rather than sending her to Atlanta or Augusta, the hospital beamed up a specialist at the Medical College of Georgia in Augusta, whose examination of the lesion via videoconferencing identified the problem as a staph infection. He prescribed a long dose of antibiotics, and the woman did not have to lose her leg. Although the 1980s doctor in California found the answer to his problem with a computer database, in this case the medical school dermatologist was able to see the wound and make a quick diagnosis in real time. The computer brought the contact between patient and doctor at a distance up close and personal.

Patients themselves are getting in the act of understanding their symptoms and drugs with so-called "doc-in-a-box" software kits and on-line support groups and forums. A woman in Wisconsin having complications from breast cancer surgery joined the growing CHESS (the Comprehensive Health Enhancement Support System) computer network at the suggestion of her hospital and found lots of advice from fellow patients with similar problems regarding her illness and medicines. CompuServe, an on-line computer information service, has a forum where patients can log on and ask questions, which are often answered by doctors. "Doc-in-a-box" software CD-ROMs, expected to be a $500 million industry by 1996, package information in multimedia that can be accessed after a patient types in a set of symptoms. The program then responds with a set of possible diagnoses and an encyclopedia article on each condition. Also included is information about thousands of drugs and medical procedures. As a cost-saving measure, some HMO plans are training nurses to use software of this kind to make preliminary diagnoses over a toll-free phone line. With computer assistance patients get advice in an impersonal and anonymous way, and studies indicate that those who have logged on tend to like it. Yet software creators and forum organizers emphasize that these approaches are meant to supplement regular medical care, not replace it.

Keeping accurate records on hospital patients is essential; but for nurses, the load of paperwork can be overwhelming. Many hospitals have installed a portable computer in patient rooms for encoding data like temperature and pulse rate as they are gathered. Using a barcode scanner, nurses can read drug and food requirements encoded on patients' armtags. Because the workstations are networked throughout the hospital, medical departments like radiology can file test results electronically as they are completed, and they are instantly available in any room. Treatment documentation and accounting records are also on-line. Errors due to illegible handwriting or verbal misunderstandings can be avoided, since the patient's master record is stored in typed form in the hospital's main computer. Not only does the networked hospital have more accurate records quickly accessible, but recordkeeping is more economical as well.

Hospitals routinely employ computer monitoring of critically ill patients when nurses are otherwise engaged. In intensive care units, for example, patients are wired with electronic sensors that monitor their vital signs, such as heartbeat and temperature. This information is collected continuously and automatically transmitted to the nurses' station, where it is displayed on a computer screen. If some vital sign falls outside the normal range, the machine beeps a warning. For example, if a heart patient's pulse falls suddenly, the machine alerts the nurse on duty, who can then respond immediately. In applications like this, the computer allows an instant diagnosis not available by other methods and can truly be a lifesaver.

Medical technology based in computers has added new diagnosis tools unimaginable only a few years ago. The most well-known one is probably computerized axial tomography, better known as the CAT or CT scanner. Today hospitals regularly use such devices to find brain tumors and other cancers and later to check for recurrence after surgery or chemotherapy. The equipment blends x-ray with computer graphic imagery techniques. The machinery takes a series of x-ray photo cuts through the bodily area under study, at slightly different angles.

The computer then merges these separate images and displays them graphically on a color screen, showing different kinds of body tissue in different colors. Magnetic resonance imaging (MRI scanning) employs a similar technology using the interaction of radio waves with hydrogen nuclei in water and fatty tissue in the body to get safe and reliable computer images of the internal organs (Redington and Berninger). With both machines, doctors have a picture of the body through computer imaging that was not possible with earlier diagnostic tools.

Computers are being used creatively to assist handicapped people through electronic prosthetics, or the replacement of missing body parts with artificial limbs or organs. Programming a computer to control artificial limbs falls into the category of cybernetics. The early computer pioneer and mathematician Norbert Wiener, of MIT, coined the term from the Greek word kybernetes, meaning "pilot" or "helmsman," to refer to the study of control mechanisms, both in animals and machines. Suppose a person has been in a car accident and lost the lower part of her left leg; yet the nerve endings are still active. Medical researchers can produce an artificial leg with computer chips that sense nerve signals to move or bend the leg. When the woman wants to walk, her brain signals the sensor on the prosthetic leg; it receives the message and moves the appropriate parts of the leg and foot. Research in cybernetics is producing wonderful progress in prothestics, helping handicapped persons and accident victims to restore bodily functions like walking and talking.

Ordinary personal computers are already working wonders for handicapped people. Voice synthesizers, chin switches, head pointers, and braille printers have opened up communications for handicapped students not even imagined a few years ago. The mouse, which users roll around on the table to select items on the computer screen, has become an input device for people who cannot use a pencil or a keyboard. A Swedish computer science student paralyzed from the shoulders down uses a head pointer, which monitors his head movements, to choose options on Macintosh menus. He then activates the option he wants with a puff switch, into which he blows a puff of breath. On a special machine that emulates a keyboard, controllable from his head pointer, he picks out a character and types it with the puff switch. The student has already developed a typing speed of 100 keystrokes per minute.

Hypermedia tools that open windows and present text, graphics, and sound with the click of a button are now accessible to people who do the clicking with a chin switch and a nod of their head. Speech recognition packages allow blind students to control their machines with their own voices. Many of these hardware options can be added to standard machines without enormous cost. Liz Vantrease, an active composer of opera and other music who has slowly debilitating Lou Gehrig's disease, has called the computer "an empowering device" for the disabled: "It can give you back some of the things that were so unfairly stolen from you by illness, accident, or birth defect". The computer extends a handicapped person's sensory and motor abilities and thus makes life more truly manageable.

In the traditional sciences, a variety of applications that depend first on the computer as a very fast and accurate calculating engine and then as a powerful graphic imaging system. These fields apply principles of mathematics to real-world applications, often using differential equations to model natural processes. Today supercomputers and high-powered graphical workstations are the staple tools of the research scientist.

Supercomputers, the most expensive computers in the world, come in different configurations, but they share one common trait: the ability to do repetitive mathematical calculations at incredible speeds. Their speed and power is usually measured in gigaflops (GFLOPs), billions of floating point (mathematical) instructions per second. Newer supercomputers have now reached peak speeds of a trillion floating point operations per second, called teraflop (TFLOP), a thousand-fold improvement over a gigaflop machine.

Weather forecasting is an everyday instance of supercomputing. Accurate weather prediction depends on the collection of temperature, wind velocity, and air pressure readings from many stations. For decades scientists have known that solving a series of complex mathematical equations containing data from thousands of weather stations will give an accurate forecast. The problem has been that the number of calculations required to solve the equations is so large. By the time they are solved by ordinary methods, the weather has changed. In the early days of computing, the first practical use of the formulas became possible. Accurate one-day forecasts were calculated with the computational power of mainframe computers of that era.

In computational science, then, the scientist can now gain insight into real-world processes not possible with earlier technologies. In this new endeavor, computer science is viewed as more than a service field that produces powerful pictures. It is central to the initial mathematical modeling of real-world phenomena and to the visual understanding of the numerical outcomes.

Suppose a scientist wants to display a moving color image on a computer screen made up of more than 1 million spots of color, called pixels, that change shade at least 15 times a second. The computational power required to calculate 15 million changes and send them to the screen in one second is a job for a supercomputer or a high-end workstation. Without such capability the researcher cannot see what is happening in real time, as the event is happening. With the computer imaging, the response seems instantaneous to the user, because human speeds of perception are much slower than computer calculations.

This sort of scientific computing is very expensive. In fact, the US National Science Foundation program of funding five National Centers for Supercomputer Applications had a budget of about $100 million a year through 1995. Supercomputing centers tend to be joint projects of universities and research institutes, which share the computational resources and costs. Thus the third of our reasons for computing, economics, joins the other two, insight and feasibility, in the explosion of scientific research through supercomputers and visualization.

Computers in the Media

Television viewers of the mid-1980s remember the clever series of Coca-Cola ads featuring the talking head Max Headroom, a personality who existed only as a disembodied image on a TV screen. Max became so popular that an ABC series was built around his adventures "twenty minutes in the future" (Fisher). The show featured hip humor, quick cinematic cutting and music, and, for the first time on network television, integrated computer graphics. Computer-generated images moved behind Max, who appeared himself to be a computer image, but was in actuality an actor made up to look like a digital creation. The result was a series about a telegenic society of constant, multiple intrusions of media into daily life. Max Headroom was not the first use of computer video in movies, but it did break ground in network television. Today even local TV stations employ easy-to-use video graphics technology for special effects in production and advertising.

Print Journalism

Computers are now an integral part of journalism and the print media. In fact, desktop publishing has changed forever the production of newspapers and magazines. "Hot type" newspaper pages, produced in the past with Linotype machines and cases of leaded type, have been replaced with cold type, the production of typefonts and pages on computer screens. Printed by laser and xerographic processes, cold type is not limited to black and white, but appears increasingly in color. The costs are lower, the range of printing possibilities is far greater, the time lag is shorter from layout to printing, and the whole enterprise can be controlled in an editorial office.

Newspaper reporters regularly carry portable laptop computers on assignment. Thousands of reporters write their stories in the field and send them back to the home office via the built-in modem and communications software in the computer. In the newsroom, staff reporters use networked terminals to check facts and produce their stories. The managing editor can call up their stories on his terminal and edit them for final printing.

Computer Graphics

In the layout department, workers use desktop publishing software to set up the pages of the paper, including the mix of stories, graphics, and digitized photographic images that make up a newspaper page. By 1990 the Dallas Times Herald included between 20 and 30 illustrations a day created on a Macintosh, along with advertising photographs that had been computer-enhanced with graphics packages. The director of computer imaging reported a doubling of computer-produced illustrations in one year, at no increase in labor or production costs (Matazzoni).

The San Francisco Examiner went high-tech when Soviet President Gorbachev visited the Bay Area in June 1990 to meet the very short deadlines of its midday and afternoon editions. Technicians videotaped Gorbachev's arrival at the Russian consulate from a television set; transferred a single frame of the tape to the newspaper's "electronic darkroom" software, run on a Macintosh; enhanced the image to print quality; and in a few minutes had the color photo on press. For later editions a reporter snapped pictures with a new Sony digital camera, which records photos on floppy diskettes rather than print film. These were easily processed in the electronic darkroom, and the final afternoon editions carried photos of Gorbachev taken that morning, before he left the area. Both technologies achieved record speed for color photography in the production process (San Francisco Examiner).

Surely one of the most well-known high-tech success stories for computers in the newspaper business is USA Today, the flashy national paper delivered daily across the country. Since it began in 1981, USA Today has been produced with computer graphics and four-color printing. Like the San Francisco Examiner, the paper began capturing photo images from television in 1990, using software called Adobe Photoshop, developed by the company that led the rush to laser printing with its PostScript software (Adobe Systems). Before printing, these digital TV photos can be edited and enhanced.

More amazing is the paper's nationwide printing process, based on satellite distribution of digitized pages. Copy for the paper is sent out every night from Washington headquarters to printing locations all over the nation. First the print pages are digitized with computer hardware; then the digitized images are sent out to the printing sites via satellite. A black-and-white page takes 3 minutes to transmit; color pages, richer in digitized information, take about 6 minutes. The printers receive the images from the satellite dishes and recreate and print the pages between midnight and 2 a.m., and the paper is available all over the country that morning. Here is an application not feasible without computer technology for digitization of images and data communication by satellites. The result is the first truly nationwide daily English language newspaper (Korzenlowski).

In a society as large as the United States, computers have been used since their earliest days to keep track of data of all kinds. Herman Hollerith, working for the Census Bureau, invented the punch card to carry out the 1890 census; UNIVAC I, the first commercial computer, helped with the 1950 count. Based on 1980 census figures, Kenneth C. Laudon described the massive numbers of people about whom records are now being kept by government and quasi-governmental agencies:

At last count there were 50 million Social Security beneficiaries, 95 million individual and 75 million business taxpayers, 21.2 million recipients of food stamps, 10.6 million recipients of Aid to Families with Dependent Children (AFDC), 24 million criminals and 60 million civilians with fingerprints at the FBI, 3.9 million elderly receiving Supplemental Security Income (SSI), 21.4 million recipients of Medicaid, 61.8 million people covered by private health plans, more than 500,000 doctors and dentists who generated 1.1 million office visits, 49.8 million public school students, 9.5 million arrests, 294,000 people in jail, 5.8 million defense industry workers, 2 million members of the armed forces, 36 million living veterans of all wars, 51 million credit card holders, 62 million credit records held in private credit data systems, 154 million registered motor vehicles, and 140 million licensed drivers.

Whereas a little more than $15 billion went into federal information technology in fiscal year 1987-88, the latest figures for 1994-95 show an investment of about $25 billion a year. Certainly the number of microcomputers the federal government owns continues to grow, but they have no current figures for state and local jurisdictions. Governments at all levels use computers to function more efficiently, effectively, and even more democratically. Computers seek out waste and fraud in government programs. They help to streamline operations by merging information collected from different agencies, for better planning, allocation of resources, and distribution of services. They work to collect taxes fairly and to discover cheaters, as well as to distribute monies to the less privileged members of the society. They use information collected about the economy and the society to make plans for future growth and development. They monitor criminal activity and seek out lawbreakers.

In addition, the federal government uses computers for our collective defense. Federal agencies reporting the most computers in 1985 were the Defense Department (66 percent of the mainframes and 39 percent of the micros in the federal government), the Department of Energy, including nuclear regulation (10 percent of the mainframes), the Justice Department, including the FBI (10 percent of the micros), and the Treasury Department, including the Internal Revenue System (4 percent of the mainframes and 6 percent of the micros).

Studies of the effects of increasing computer usage in government have focused discussion among constitutional scholars on the shifting divisions of power among the three branches of the federal government, and on the power relations between the federal government and the states. One question concerns the computer's role in bringing about unequal parity in the historical checks and balances embodied in the Constitution among governmental bodies. The agencies that possess most of the federal government's computers are departments of the executive branch, controlled by Cabinet members. With this massive control over computer information resources, the president and the executive branch seem to have an unfair advantage in the distribution of power.

In US, since the early 1970s, congress added its own considerable computer resources—for example, for modeling the federal budget process in the Congressional Budget Office. It regularly requires the executive branch to share its computer-produced materials for consideration in the legislative process. Since the election of 1994, the continuing battle between the Republican Congress and the Democratic White House has reached onto the Internet. Before the election, the White House went onto the World Wide Web with one of the most popular home pages: http://www.whitehouse.gov. Visitors can not only view photos of the mansion but also position papers from the Clinton administration. Similarly most executive department agencies have added Web sites with the strong encouragement of the Clinton-Gore administration.

The judiciary, the least computerized of the three branches, can also require information from the executive departments, and has the power to rule ineligible whatever evidence it chooses. In other words, the judiciary can decide in particular cases whether information is or is not relevant and thus may stymie the executive branch's arguments by ruling its massive data files inadmissible to the case at hand. Computers have only intensified the continual tug of war for power between the branches of the federal government.

In relations between the federal government and the states and cities, the evidence is more mixed. Especially in social welfare and law enforcement, the federal government has more presence on the local level now than ever before. With the provision of welfare funds from states and national agencies to cities and counties come mandates about how the programs must be administered and monitored. This degree of governmental control is made possible with computers; whether it is desirable is a controversial political issue.

Computers in Defence

Certainly the most massive use and expenditure on computers in the U.S. government has been in defense of the nation. The famous and controversial Star Wars weapons program of the 1980s, properly called the Strategic Defense Initiative (SDI), was based on the use of computers to monitor attacking missiles and automatically deploy defensive missiles to destroy them. The program has been vilified by some computer professionals as too expensive and unworkable, and credited by supporters with helping to end the Cold War (because the Soviet Union had neither the technology nor the finances to mount a credible alternative). Some critics alleged that SDI was far more than a defensive system and could be used for a preemptive first-strike nuclear attack.

Star Wars aside, modern warfare was changed forever by the so-called smart weapons that aided soldiers, sailors, and pilots in the 1991 Persian Gulf War, which has been called "the first information war" by author Alan Campen. High-tech successes included Tomahawk stealth missiles, which sought out and destroyed their targets with pinpoint accuracy, and Patriot missiles, which used computer-generated trajectories to intercept incoming Iraqi Scuds. In a continuing research project called the supercockpit, pilots wear "virtual reality helmets." As in a video game, computers in the helmets show pilots the terrain ahead of them, the enemy weapons approaching, and the evasive actions they can take. Research includes voice-control systems that allow planes to be flown by speech commands. If the pilot is unable to fly the plane, the computer, dubbed the "pilot's associate," takes over .

War is becoming depersonalized; the enemy is not seen by the soldier or the pilot, but found and destroyed electronically. Even in the ranks of defense analysts, critics contend that General George Patton was right when he said, "Wars may be fought with weapons, but they are won by men. It is the spirit of men who follow and of the man who leads that gains the victory." A lot of faith and federal research money have been invested in the Strategic Computing Program of the Defense Department and in the workability of automated weapons. Whether defense budgets will be able to keep pace with the 1980s in these times of federal deficits and the end of the Cold War, in order to sustain the research required by these new computing systems, remains an important question for national debate among Congress and the American people.

Index